PHILIP'S

WELSH
BORDERS

LANDSCAPE · ARCHITECTURE · HISTORY

PHILIP'S
WELSH BORDERS

LANDSCAPE · ARCHITECTURE · HISTORY

CHRISTOPHER SOMERVILLE

PHOTOGRAPHY BY JOHN HESELTINE

GEORGE
PHILIP

For Elizabeth and Mary – future explorers
of these Borders

Contrasting textures of stone,
timber and plaster in houses at Much
Wenlock, Shropshire (HALF-TITLE PAGE),
and the patchwork of sheep-cropped slopes
and valley fields with the mountains rising
beyond (TITLE PAGE), *near Abergavenny,*
Gwent, both perfectly express the Welsh
Borders. Their quietly undemonstrative
beauty is filled with sudden views, small
and proud market towns, the strength of
once-defiant castles and the pathos of
abandoned abbeys, and with houses,
churches and byways which time
seems almost to have
passed by.

First published by George Philip Limited,
59 Grosvenor Street, London W1X 9DA

Text © Christopher Somerville 1991
Photographs © John Heseltine 1991
Maps © George Philip 1991
Based upon the Ordnance Survey maps with the permission
of Her Majesty's Stationery Office
© Crown copyright

British Library Cataloguing in Publication Data

Somerville, Christopher
    The Welsh Borders. — (Philip's travel guides)
    1. England. Wales. Travel
    I. Title
    914.2404859

ISBN 0-540-01245-9

Maps by John Gilkes
Typeset by Keyspools Limited, Golborne, Lancs
Printed in Italy

Contents

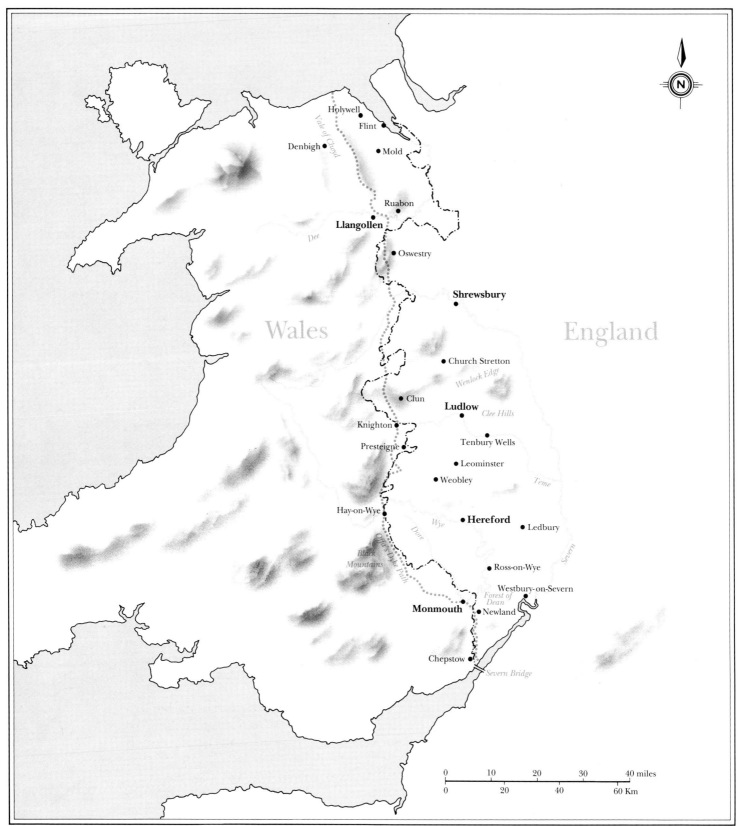

Holywell
Flint
Denbigh
Mold
Vale of Clwyd
Ruabon
Llangollen
Dee
Oswestry
Shrewsbury
Wales
England
Church Stretton
Wenlock Edge
Clun
Ludlow
Clee Hills
Knighton
Tenbury Wells
Presteigne
Leominster
Weobley
Teme
Hay-on-Wye
Wye
Hereford
Ledbury
Dore
Black Mountains
Offa's Dyke Path
Ross-on-Wye
Severn
Westbury-on-Severn
Forest of Dean
Monmouth
Newland
Chepstow
Severn Bridge

0	10	20	30	40 miles
0	20	40		60 Km

Introduction

The Welsh Borders can be driven by an impatient motorist from one end to the other in a single morning. But their subtle delights are better savoured by travellers with a relaxed timetable and no fixed objectives in mind. There is a particularly seductive slackening of tension among those deep valleys and rolling hills, a feeling of time running thick and slow. The landscape itself is consistently beautiful, be it the hard-edged drama of the Black Mountains, the Kerry Hills and the Stiperstones of Shropshire, or the pastoral softness of the wide lowland valleys around Leominster. There is endless variety in the towns and villages, from the half-timbered charm of magpie showpieces such as Weobley and Ludlow to the wind-bitten starkness of the moorland mining villages in the Clee Hills and on Halkyn Mountain near the Clwyd coast. There are historic buildings as well known as Hereford Cathedral, Powis Castle and Llanthony Priory, and as obscure as the 800-year-old mill at Limebrook (see p. 107) which could feature, just as it stands, in any Brueghel painting. All these you will discover on the five tours suggested in this book. As for the people of the Welsh Borders, I know of nowhere in Britain where you are more likely to ask a sheep farmer a straightforward road direction and find yourself, half an hour later, still hanging over the field gate yarning away. On the heights of the Black Mountains and in the depths of the Forest of Dean there are people living what the twentieth century might be pleased to call an outmoded way of life – old-fashioned, perhaps; certainly idiosyncratic and impenetrable to the 'foreigner'.

Foreignness on the Welsh Borders is very much a matter of local culture rather than of national identity. There is little or none of the Welsh/English antipathy found further to the west, though plenty of pride in one's own side. Every Borderer is a foreigner to some extent, enriched by a mixture of cultural influences from both east and west. Welsh Border history is strong stuff indeed, a cocktail of repression, resistance, pride and terrible bloodshed. Without some grasp of its outline you will be blind and deaf to a large part of all the Borders have to offer.

The Romans made little headway into Wales, and little impression on the Borders. It was the Anglo-Saxons who succeeded in pinning back the Welsh Britons behind a more or less fixed boundary. In doing so they lit the touchpaper of nearly 1000 years of militant nationalism. But the real trouble began with the Normans. The story of their attempts, and the attempts of their successors, to subdue the Welsh dominates the history of the Borders from the time of the Norman Conquest until the collapse of Owain Glyndŵr's rebellion 350 years later. All up the great sweep of the Borders you will come across the ruins of the castles from which successive English kings and their barons

The mud and rocks of the River Severn which has one of the largest tidal ranges in the world, are exposed at low tide near Westbury, Gloucestershire. Routes through the Borders cross and recross the Severn.

launched sorties, sallies, expeditions and full-blown invasions into Wales. Any exploration of the Welsh Borders brings you face to face with the facts, the tales and legends, the horrifying cruelties and brave convictions of those troubled centuries.

The central figures were the Lords Marcher, whose power and position were established by William the Conqueror (1066–87) soon after his victory at Hastings. It was an excellent way of killing two awkward birds with one stone – to occupy his most warlike and potentially troublesome barons in bringing to heel the most turbulent of his new subjects. Within 30 years or so there were around 140 Lords of the Marches ('march' meaning simply 'border'), each based in his own motte-and-bailey stronghold, each running his own patch as a private kingdom – in theory answerable to the Crown, but in practice answerable to no-one. The Border lords squabbled and feuded, fought and raided and forged alliances through marriage with each other and with noble Welsh families. They consolidated their positions as immensely powerful autocrats, and kept hold of their privileges until in 1536 Henry VIII's Act of Union between England and Wales cut them all down like so much dead wood.

Against this continuous background the main historical players acted out the milestone events of Border history. During the twelfth century the Norman barons, with the blessing of Henry I (1100–35), pushed far into Wales, grabbing land as they went. While King Stephen (1135–54) was preoccupied with his civil war the Welsh retook a good deal of it. Henry II (1154–89) took it back again, and built the first Border castles of stone to help him keep it. By the end of the century the Welsh were more or less united under Prince Llewelyn the Great (1173–1240), a ruler powerful and energetic enough to bring most of Wales and the Borders back under his control in the first half of the thirteenth century, and to force both King John (1199–1216) and Henry III (1216–72) to respect him and his influence. His grandson Llewelyn the Last dominated Wales for much of the latter half of that century, driving the English out of his lands and gaining recognition from Henry III of his right to the title of Prince of Wales.

But even Prince Llewelyn was no match for the single-minded drive of Edward I (1272–1307) when he succeeded to the English throne . The 'Hammer of the Scots' proved to be an irresistible battering-ram of the Welsh as well. Within ten years all Welsh dreams of autonomy had been ruthlessly stamped out, and a new chain of immensely strong stone castles laid along the Borders. Llewelyn had been killed in a skirmish, a refugee fleeing for his life, while his brother Dafydd, last pretender to the throne of Wales, had met a horrible end at the hands of the Shrewsbury executioners. Welsh nationalism was down and apparently out, and it remained dormant all through the fourteenth century – dormant, but not extinct.

There was a final flare-up in 1400, when the charismatic prince Owain Glyndŵr (c.1354–c.1416) drove his rebellion like fire along the Borders, sacking towns and slaughtering the English and their sympathizers. Welsh resentment, which had been quietly simmering for a hundred years, roared high to fuel Glyndŵr's progress for a few headlong years. Henry IV (1399–1413) could not control him. It was left to the king's son, dashing Prince Hal of Monmouth, to bring the rebels finally to heel and force Glyndŵr into hiding as an outlaw. The great Welsh leader met an obscure, unrecorded death in about 1416, and with him died the last hopes of Welshmen for an independent Wales.

At the end of it all, life in the Borders was much as it had been all along – still dominated by the Lords Marcher and those from the east. The Welsh gentry entered a period of quarantine that lasted well over a century: no public office allowed, no power, little land or money. But they did see one of their own countrymen at last ascend a throne, even if it was that of England – Henry Tudor, the exile who returned to take the crown and found a dynasty at Bosworth Field. And it was his son, Henry VIII (1509–47), who unified the two countries in 1536, brought the Welsh in out of the cold and back into public life again, and abolished the Lords Marcher and all their power. Apart from the skirmishes and regional blood-lettings of the Civil War (during which the Borders were mostly for the king, and duly suffered for their loyalty) peace descended, never again to be broken. But if those centuries of turmoil seem not to have scarred the Border psyche, they have certainly left their mark on the landscape in the shape of castles, town gates and walls, battlefields, and churches like fortresses with doorless towers built for refuge.

To one question there is no clear answer – where exactly *are* the Welsh Borders? All one can say with certainty is that they encompass two boundaries – the present-day political border between England and Wales, and the great snaking earthwork of Offa's Dyke. Offa, King of Mercia (AD 757–96), built his dyke some time between AD 778 and 796 as a border marker giving unimpeded views west into the territory of his potential enemies, the Welsh. The dyke itself runs south to north across country for some 80 miles (128 km); the Long-Distance Footpath established along its line is more than double that length as it stretches from the Bristol Channel to the Dee estuary. In many ways it offers the best – some would say the only proper – way to explore Welsh Border country. Several side-tracks along Offa's Dyke are suggested in the following tours, and you will undoubtedly find many others for yourself. But just how far the Borders extend each side of the dyke and the political boundary is a matter of feeling and intuition. I have taken a very loose framework which leans up against the first serious rise of the Welsh hills on the west, and straggles out towards the River Severn on the east. Anything within these bounds, and a good deal outside them at various points, I have considered fair game, making my own personal judgement about where English or Welsh influence becomes too strong for true Border country. But there is nothing definitive about these boundaries.

Four of the five tour bases – Monmouth, Hereford, Ludlow and Shrewsbury – are recognized as the social and commercial centres of their respective regions. The fifth, Llangollen, though a small town, is situated at the meeting place of several sorts of Border landscape. From each of these bases I have devised a tangled spider's web of a tour, leading you not just to the most exciting, historic and beautiful places, but up many a side turning and blind alley where something good and unexpected waits round a corner. If these tours stimulate you to turn off along the side roads that I have not mentioned, to find the country pubs and restaurants that have slipped through my net, to enjoy the conversations that I never had, then I shall have done what I set out to do, and you will find yourself as thoroughly seduced as I have been by the timeless delights of the Welsh Borders.

Many ancient churches survive in the Welsh Borders, some sheltered beneath the protection of a once-great castle, like the little church at Skenfrith, Gwent (ABOVE), *and many with the proud and exuberant decoration of later Norman stonework, such as the deeply cut dogstooth and the layer upon layer of arches forming the west door into Chepstow church, Gwent.*

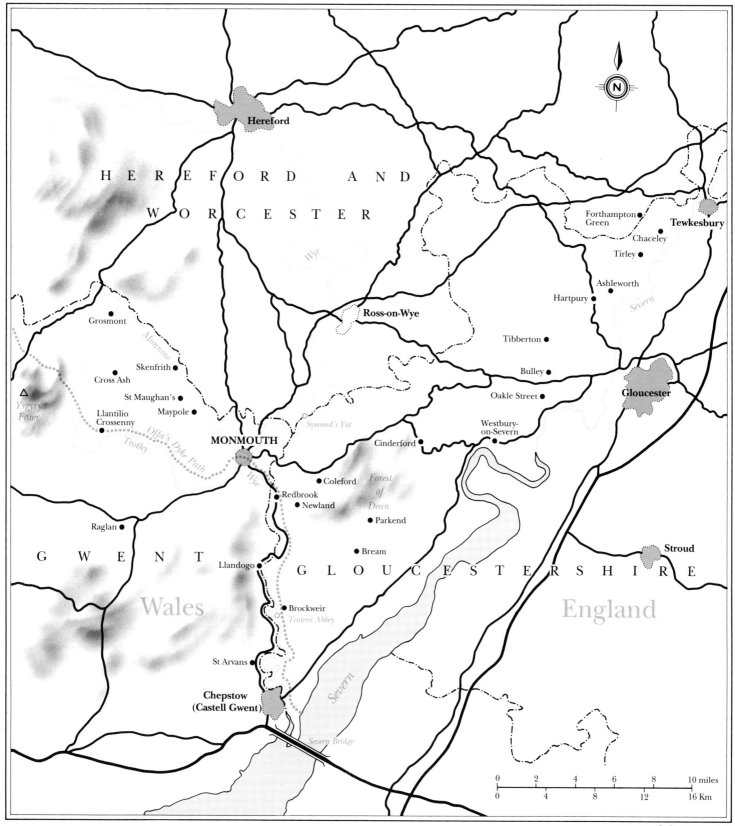

© Crown copyright

12

1

Monmouth and the Forest of Dean

MONMOUTH · THREE CASTLES · RAGLAN · CHEPSTOW
TINTERN · FOREST OF DEAN · WESTBURY-ON-SEVERN
ROSS-ON-WYE · SYMOND'S YAT

Monmouth is very much a typical Welsh Borders town, and the sheep market on the bank of the River Monnow at the southern edge of the town is as good a place as any to catch an instant flavour of that meeting of Welsh and English influences which colours every aspect of a journey along the Borders. Here the hill farmers, summoned from the cafés and pubs by a handbell rung around the streets, gather round the pens to pinch sheep tails and squeeze fleeces while the auctioneer chants his litany: 'Two-forty, two-forty, I-got-you-Evan, two-sixty, two-sixty, at-two-pound-sixty, are-we-all-done?' The sheep, their ears bloodied by the auctioneer's punch, wait dully for the Land Rovers and trailers to carry them off to pastures on either side of the border.

Conversation among the watchful purchasers jumps and rings with Welsh intonation and idiom. Yet under those expressive Welsh tones lie the burr and rumble of rural Gloucestershire and Herefordshire. Little Welsh is spoken in the market and round the streets of Monmouth; it's English spiced with Welsh . The town itself stands solidly within Wales, though only by a couple of miles. Before the present county of Gwent in which it lies was formed in 1974, the county of Monmouthshire had been technically a part of England for more than four hundred years, but its atmosphere and sense of itself are Welsh through and through. No-one coming to Monmouth and using their ears and eyes could doubt that the town looks west rather than east, or that the majority of its visiting shoppers, marketers and idlers come from hill farms and villages to the west of the River Wye. Like all Border towns, Monmouth has been much fought-over in the nine centuries since the Normans laid it out above the flood line of the Monnow. They chose a raised terrace in a peninsular loop of the river close to its junction with the larger River Wye – an important defensive site, guarding two vital river routes into the heart of southern Wales. Monmouth was destined to pass frequently between Welsh and English hands – three or four times in the thirteenth century alone – before Edward I, as part of

Caught in the embrace of the River Monnow, and with little growth beyond its ancient boundaries, Monmouth (Gwent) now stands firmly in Wales, although its old county, Monmouthshire, always had an anomalous position.

his monumentally successful campaign to crush Welsh insurgency in the 1270s and 1280s, added the old princedom of Gwent to England. But the town remained the base of a Marcher Lordship, one of those almost independent Border states ruled so ruthlessly and autocratically by their lords, until 1536 and the Acts of Union between England and Wales, when it came under the English umbrella and out of the stormy disputes of Border history.

Beyond the market pens the Norman town site looks through the narrow peephole of the gatehouse on Monnow Bridge – the only fortified bridge left in Britain – south-west across the river to the even older settlement of Over Monnow. The church of St Thomas Becket in Over Monnow has a superb Norman chancel arch with clear-cut chevron carving; but what is now a pleasant suburb of Monmouth, with old houses on winding side lanes, was probably a thriving village when its big sister town was not even a twinkle in a Norman eye. The Romans had their settlement of Blestium here, and it's likely that people have been going about their business in Over Monnow continuously for at least 2000 years. The old gatehouse, built against the threat of Welsh attack in 1270, stands astride the narrow Monnow Bridge; its slim archway is less than 10 feet (3 m) wide and before the Monmouth bypass was built was a notorious bottleneck for through traffic between England and Wales.

From the gatehouse Monnow Street rises, a wide thoroughfare narrowing as it slopes up to the centre of Monmouth, the cobbled Agincourt Square with its big old hotels and comfortable market town pubs. The King's Head is a large, rambling old

The statues of the warrior Henry V and of the aviation and motoring pioneer Charles Rolls, two of Monmouth's most famous sons, stand facing into Agincourt Square, named after the young king's great victory of 1415.

place, built and still maintained for quiet ease; the bar has a fine painted roundel of fruit and flowers in the ceiling, and a carving of King Charles over the fireplace with bulging eyes and a cheery half-smile. In the Punch House Inn you can eat salmon from the River Wye in the first-floor restaurant, or eavesdrop on local gossip in the often jam-packed bar. The Beaufort Arms, where Lord Nelson stayed in 1802 on his fact-finding mission to learn about the Forest of Dean's timber industry, is no longer a hotel; but its courtyard has become a pretty shopping mews.

The centre of Agincourt Square is filled by the pale stone bulk of the early Georgian Shire Hall. In a niche in the front of the building stands a statue of the victor of Agincourt, Henry V (1413–22), with a stubby little torso and oversized, ape-like arms. Henry was born in Monmouth Castle in 1387, his mother a member of the Norman de Bohun family, Earls of Hereford and very influential in Border politics. The young Prince Hal felt strong ties of affection with his birthplace, and as a warrior king had many bowmen of Monmouth with him at Agincourt in 1415. He stares out at the traffic over the head of a statue to another of Monmouth's famous sons, the motoring and flying pioneer, the Hon. Charles Stewart Rolls (1877–1910). C.S. Rolls was already a well-known figure in the early motoring world when he formed the Rolls-Royce firm with Henry Royce in 1904 – he had bought his first car back in 1895 at the age of 18, the fourth person in England to own one. Rolls died in an air crash in 1910, aged 32, but by then his engineering experiments and his frontier-breaking spirit had ensured his fame. His statue is an altogether better job than that of King Henry. On a plinth showing some of his exploits (a balloon ascent, a car race, an aeroplane flight), Rolls stands in romantic early flying gear, a scarf wrapped over his ears, looking proudly at a model of a biplane in his hand.

Castle Hill leads out of the west side of Agincourt Square and up to the ruined walls of Monmouth Castle, built soon after the Norman Conquest by one of the founders of the Marcher Lordship of Gwent, William FitzOsbern. Prince Hal's birthplace is a sad ruin nowadays; a far more impressive building, Great Castle House, stands opposite, built by the 3rd Marquess of Worcester in 1673 as a fine historical flourish – he wanted his first grandson to be born on the same site as Prince Hal. It's a florid-faced, imposing house, giving Monmouth Castle a continuing toehold in military matters as the headquarters of the Royal Monmouthshire Royal Engineers.

From the eastern side of Agincourt Square, narrow Church Street, now paved and pedestrianized, runs between attractive old shops and houses. It's hard to believe that this was once the main road into Monmouth. Church Street opens out into the elegance of Whitecross Street where local gentry built their fine houses in Monmouth's Georgian heyday as a wintering town where parties, concerts, balls and visiting kept the January and February blues away. The church of St Mary stands here, its slender 200-foot (61-m) spire soaring above the houses, enticing passers-by into what turns out to be an over-restored interior oppressed by a darkly lowering timber roof. Better to stroll on down Whitecross Street and out into the open space of St James's Square, rather off the usual visitors' beat, a quiet green triangle surrounded by colour-washed old houses. In the middle of the green grows a large and beautiful catalpa or Indian Bean tree with big papery leaves flicking in the breeze, while in the background swells the wooded dome of Kymin Hill. It's well worth putting aside a couple of hours to cross the River Wye (the Wye Bridge is just below you here) and climb the steepish path up to the bald crown of Kymin Hill. This is National Trust land, with a really fine view from 840 feet (256 m)

Steps ascend to the entrance of Great Castle House, built in 1673 on the site of the old Monmouth Castle, a tall town house in a provincial version of the prevailing post-Restoration style.

down over Monmouth and the Wye Valley, both north and south, as well as east to the green waves of the Forest of Dean. On the top of Kymin Hill the Georgian gentlemen and ladies of the Kymin Club laid out a little walking park for themselves and built a Banqueting Pavilion for their own regular summertime feasts-with-a-view, as well as a Naval Temple to the glory of English sea victories. The round, battlemented pavilion is now part of a private house, and the ugly little temple stands forlorn like a pretentious municipal bus shelter. It was a grander affair when opened in 1801 with feasting and dancing. Round the tops of its walls are medallions commemorating great English admirals and their victories, including Boscawen (Lagos Bay, 1759), Hawke (Quiberon Bay, 1759), Hood (Toulon, 1793), Nelson (the Nile, 1798), Parker (Copenhagen, 1801). Triumphs over French, Spanish, Dutch and Danish enemies are celebrated – Britain against the civilized world, no less.

Back in St James's Square, the Nag's Head on the corner makes a clean, unfussy and friendly place to rest a while. Then you walk back by Whitecross Street and the eastern end of St Mary's church to reach a crossroads from which the Hereford road, known as Monk Street, runs north. A stroll up Monk Street will take you past many fine old buildings, none more piquant than the present Masonic Hall, just over the crossroads on the left. There are Masonic symbols – compasses and squares – over the side doors of the hall, but before the Masons took it over in 1837 it had housed forty years of different rituals as the town's theatre.

St Mary's was the church of Monmouth's priory, founded in the early twelfth century and now all but vanished. Priory Street, old though its name sounds, was built during the last century to relieve the pressure of through traffic on the tight-waisted Church Street. You can return in two minutes to Agincourt Square by way of Priory Street, but make extra time to delve into the steeply sloping little side cut on the right which leads down to the great archways that underlie Priory Street, looking out over the River Monnow to green playing fields and tree-covered hills. Inside the sandstone arches are relics for the unsqueamish of a seldom-trumpeted aspect of Monmouth's history. Here in these damp, dank caverns were the town slaughterhouses. Some of the rotting

The oriel of the old School House, resting on corbels of overweight medieval angels and clerics, is one of the many little details that gladden the eye in the streets of Monmouth.

wooden doorways still carry their original Victorian enamel number plaques. At the back of the arches are traces of medieval stone vaulting – underground remnants of the long-vanished Priory buildings, perhaps? The floors slope down to drainholes through which the animal blood and excrement flowed to the Monnow. Some archways contain chains, pulleys, hooks and hoists for carcasses; in others are the wooden stalls and tethering rings for those about to die. Among the graffiti, some unknown dauber has executed crude modern cave paintings – men in horned hoods, chasing and spearing cattle. Though still ten minutes' walk from Monmouth's beast market where our town walk began, in this dark and grim sub-world by the river we seem to come full circle.

In its position guarding important river and land routes between England and Wales, Monmouth always had a central role in Border troubles. Three ruined castles stand round the broad base of the hill of Graig Syfyrddin to the north-west of the town, reflecting its strategic significance in the early Middle Ages. Skenfrith Castle, Grosmont Castle and White Castle, known as the 'Three Castles' or the 'Welsh Trilateral', were built by the Norman Marcher Lords to strengthen this vulnerable area against Welsh counter-attacks as the conquerors pushed ever further west beyond the Wye. The sight of their round towers and walls among the peaceful green hills and valleys of Monmouthshire is the first of a long series of castle-and-countryside images that extends the whole length of the Welsh Borders. Skenfrith is the first, reached by the B4347 and then the minor road north by way of Maypole and St Maughan's, running through wooded, rolling country of steep hillsides and deep valleys where some farms and cottages still keep their little orchards. Skenfrith Castle is a small box of shattered red sandstone walls with round turrets at each corner, standing beyond a little bridge over the River Monnow where a few houses cluster. The little ridge-top village of Grosmont, 5 winding miles (8 km) up the valley, was a thriving market town, a borough with its own fair, when Grosmont Castle stood complete and full of armed men. The layout of the village retains most of its medieval shape, with the long 'burgage plots' (land granted to the original burgesses in the early thirteenth century) now transmuted into the gardens of houses round the market place. The cruciform church of St Nicholas with its octagonal central tower shows in its size the past importance of Grosmont. These days the eastern end of the church is quite big enough to cope with local worshippers; the great Norman nave, flagged with mighty old gravestones, fell out of use long ago. Grosmont Castle stands on its mound up an unobtrusive side turning opposite the post office, its impressively tall walls and arches rising from a deep moat. From the north wall a superb fourteenth-century chimney soars almost 60 feet (18 m) into the air, crowned with a beautifully preserved little stone canopy. A stone stairway leads up to the top of the castle's west wall, from where there is a fine view over Grosmont and through the valleys running west and east below the village.

A minor road takes you south from Grosmont to turn right on the B4521 at Cross Ash. In 3 miles (5 km) the lane on the left (O.S. ref. 380180) leads to the third of the Three Castles, the best preserved, the grimmest and loneliest. The great rising keel shape of the mini-mountain of Ysgyryd Fawr dominates these valleys, and White Castle dominates its own patch above the River Trothy with its massive curtain walls and drum towers. From the top of the inner gatehouse tower and from the southern archways you can get a good idea of the castle's layout – an inner ward (defensive wall) looking south to a 'hornwork' or crescent-shaped outer earthwork in the moat, north to the spreading half-

Built to command one of the major routes between conquered England and rebellious Wales, Skenfrith Castle is the first of the now ruinous triumvirate of great Norman castles built by the Norman Marcher Lords.

circle of the outer ward. Outer ward, drum towers and gatehouses were all built in the 1260s when the rebel Earl Simon de Montfort, in alliance with Prince Llewelyn the Last and backed by many Welshmen resentful of their Marcher Lords, threatened to overthrow Henry III. White Castle must have been virtually impregnable. A market town and borough grew up in its shelter. But there is no village near the castle today – the great walls frown down on a couple of farms and an empty valley.

Two miles (3 km) south-east of White Castle, the village of Llantilio Crossenny straggles round its own little cross of roads just off the B4233. It is a small village – but with three features worth exploring. The first, Hen 'Cwrt or Old Court, lies in the angle of the B-road and lane from White Castle (395151), a square green plot of grassy ground the size of a suburban garden, surrounded by a moat full of waterlilies and rushes. Here stood the palace of the bishops of Llandaff, used by them during the Middle Ages as a temporary base when visiting their manor at Llantilio Crossenny. Nothing remains of the palace now, but there is a tradition that it passed from the bishops into the ownership of Dafydd ap Llewelyn, a fifteenth-century figure shadowed round with legend. He may have been the original model for William Shakespeare's stage Welshman, 'Fluellen valiant, and touch'd with choler, hot as gunpowder', who in *Henry V* forces a leek down the mocking Pistol's throat in revenge for an insult. Fluellen survives the Battle of Agincourt in Shakespeare's play; but the real Dafydd ap Llewelyn died there, having been knighted on the field of battle. This brave man, whose children were said to be so numerous that they could form a chain holding hands between the church door and their own front door, had a blemished or 'gammy' eye, hence his nickname of Sir David Gam.

The church of St Teilo at Llantilio Crossenny is another which is rather too big for its present-day congregation; it was built to serve as a kind of occasional cathedral for the visiting bishops of Llandaff, and shows several centuries of addition and reconstruction in its fabric. Hence the great height of the nave, dropping to a tiny chancel arch, and the lovely fourteenth-century Decorated windows of the chancel. Massive oak posts were put in early in the eighteenth century to make a solid frame in the crossing of the transepts, strengthening the tower for its then brand-new ring of six bells. At the crossroads below the church stands the Hostry Inn, a name that has stuck to successive pubs in the village for well over 500 years.

You leave Llantilio Crossenny by a lane that runs due south over a wide, stream-netted countryside to reach Raglan Castle, perched above the busy dual carriageway of the A40. The road brings clutches of tourists to Raglan Castle, a far more picturesque and scenic ruin than the Three Castles. It's bigger and better preserved, dating mostly from the fifteenth and sixteenth centuries when the turbulent eras of the Llewelyn princes and of Owain Glyndŵr had long given way to a more settled situation. During the Civil War Raglan Castle was 'slighted' or half-demolished after the Parliamentarians had captured it from the 2nd Marquess of Worcester in 1646, leaving holes all over the structure. The Great Tower and the hexagonal gatehouse towers soar high, arches leap across gaps, unbroken window frames of close-fitting masonry look down beyond vaulted roofs to smooth stone floors. Raglan Castle is a masterpiece of the stonemason's art, highly romantic and graceful, in striking contrast to its three roughly built and starkly defiant elder sisters back in the hills to the north.

The A449 and then the B4235 go south and east from Raglan, cutting across a low, wide and wooded landscape with a gentle dip and swell to it, flattening out the nearer you come to where the Wye dips its mouth in the Severn, 2 miles (3 km) wide at this point and spanned by the 5240-foot (1,600-m) Severn Bridge. Here at the confluence of Severn and Wye stands Chepstow (Castell Gwent to Welsh speakers), a town that flourished and grew prosperous on river trade under the protection of its mighty castle. Chepstow Castle really is all that a castle should be, sited in one of the most superb defensive and scenic positions imaginable, right on the rim of limestone cliffs plunging down to a sharp bend of the Wye. The whole town is on a slope of one kind or another, steep or shallow, sited on a snub, north-facing peninsular crook of the river.

From the castellated Town Gate in the centre of Chepstow substantial parts of the old Port Wall still curve round and down, to the castle on the north side of the peninsula and the river on the east, shutting off the old town in a little fortified enclave at the top of the river bend. Town Gate and Port Wall were built in the 1270s to strengthen Chepstow's defences, and their good state of preservation adds to the town's old-fashioned, enclosed feel. Moor Street comes down from on high to pass through the old stone gateway, continuing its steep slope as High Street to reach Beaufort Square half-way down the hill. The square is pleasant enough now, with its elegant Georgian buildings and open view over the lower part of the town to the opposite river cliff of the Wye: how much more charming it must have looked in the days when Chepstow market was held on its slope.

Three parallel streets run from the bottom end of Beaufort Square – St Mary Street, where the tall Beaufort Arms (an old coaching inn), makes a characterful and comfortable night's stopping place; Middle Street; and the dark, cobbled Hocker Hill Street, which slants downhill to meet Upper Church Street. Look left here to see the little right-angled courtyard of the Powis Almshouses, built in 1721 in Queen Anne style; then look right and across Upper Church Street at the rather hideously restored Montague Almshouses of 1613. Nearby Davis Court fulfils the same role on public money as its two older neighbours did for centuries on private bequests – providing sheltered accommodation for Chepstow's senior citizens.

At the far end of Upper Church Street stands St Mary's church, built from 1072 onwards as the church of the Benedictine Priory founded here by the Earl of Hereford, William FitzOsbern – he also built the castles at Chepstow and at Monmouth. St Mary's has a lovely Norman west front with many-tiered, chevroned arches, the chevrons interlaced in a Scandinavian style around the window above the west door. The church looks square and box-like, each corner and angle sharply cut; its north and south walls show forbidding stone faces with small round-topped windows like narrowed eyes. Inside, the fortress atmosphere persists: massive Norman piers under high walls pierced with two upper storeys of little round arches. Under a mat on the floor inside the west door lies the grave slab of Sir Henry Marten – the third slab to commemorate him, the other two having been scuffed into illegibility by generations of Chepstow shoes. Marten was one of the co-signatories of the death warrant of Charles I, and paid for that act with his liberty when the king's son returned to the throne in 1660. Marten spent twenty years

The holes puncturing the late medieval walls of Raglan Castle (OPPOSITE) *are the legacy of the Civil War attack leading to its capture in 1646 from the Royalists, the last in a long line of military actions on this border.*

imprisoned in various castles, Chepstow the last of them, before dying in 1680. His epitaph, an acrostic one, cocks a defiant snook at his captors:

Here or elsewhere, all's one to you, or me,
Earth, air, or water gripes my ghostless dust,
None knows how soon to be by fire set free.
Reader, if you an oft-tried rule will trust,
You'll gladly do and suffer what you must.

My life was spent with serving you and you,
And death's my pay, it seems, and welcome, too,
Revenge destroying but itself, while I
To birds of prey leave my old cage and fly.
Examples preach to the eye; care then (mine says)
Not how you end but how you spend your days.

There is an air of cool superiority about this rhyme, but Henry Marten had his hot-blooded moments, it seems. The story goes that while Oliver Cromwell was putting his signature to the king's death warrant, his nib caught in the paper and spluttered ink up into Marten's face. Marten instantly grabbed the quill and inked Cromwell's face in retaliation, something not many men would have cared to try.

Below St Mary's church are side lanes of old eighteenth- and nineteenth-century brick cottages, little changed externally over the years. Down on The Back you come to the River Wye, just upstream of where it swills below the new concrete piers of the road bridge and the old cast-iron ones of the railway bridge built by I.K. Brunel (1806–59). Strong smells of mud and salt rise from the Wye, whose fast tidal currents eddy and swirl under white limestone cliffs with tortuously snaking strata. This was once Chepstow's working waterfront where, until well into Victorian times, timber, cider, corn, coals and limestone were all loaded into ships and flat-bottomed 'trows'. Here were warehouses and mills (some now converted, a few still standing empty), quays where people from all round the Chepstow area would bring their produce to catch the boats to Bristol market, busy shipyards, fishing boat jetties and a whole maze of taverns and small shops. Chepstow was one of Britain's chief wine-importing towns in medieval days, before Henry VIII put a stop to its duty-free status. All this rich river life along the bends of the Wye has vanished entirely, killed off by changing ways. Chepstow Farmers Ltd, a brushworks, and a couple of service businesses keep a faint whiff of work about the area. A pleasant stroll upstream through peaceful Riverside Gardens (once a hammering shipyard), whose ornate bandstand is inlaid with tableaux of shipbuilding, takes you to a graceful cast-iron bridge over the Wye, built by the Scottish engineer John Rennie (1761–1821), from which there is a truly memorable view of Chepstow Castle's walls and towers curving along their clifftop eyrie above the river. This is a marvellously romantic scene, the ruined towers and square Norman keep standing guard on the wooded cliff that sweeps away round the bend of the Wye.

Chepstow Castle is the oldest stone-built castle in Britain, begun the year after the Norman Conquest, built in a unique elongated shape to fit the narrow top of the cliff. The yellow sandstone Great Tower in the centre of the range is the original castle of William

FitzOsbern, its arches, both whole and ruined, a treat for the eye; from it in the early thirteenth century the Earls of Pembroke built curtain walls to form upper, middle and lower baileys, a barbican and a great gatehouse. This is a gatehouse designed to overawe, with its crenellated towers, cross-shaped arrow slits and portcullis cavity. You half expect to see Lord and party come riding out with hawks on wrists or swords in hand. Chepstow is splendidly evocative of its medieval role, and from its windows and battlements are real castle-wall views commanding town, river and surrounding countryside.

The romantic look of Chepstow Castle had a lot to do with the popularity of the Wye Valley among eighteenth- and nineteenth-century tourists. Once the public eye had

On the bluff above the confluence of the Rivers Severn and Wye, the massive bulk of Chepstow Castle has guarded access to Wales, and helped protect the English, since the very earliest days of the Norman Conquest.

begun to regard rugged natural scenery as worthy of appreciation, the winding, wooded and cliff-bound Wye attracted visitors in their tens of thousands. Tourists would travel by boat between Chepstow and Ross-on-Wye, taking a couple of days over the journey with frequent stops to visit inns, viewpoints and local worthies. These days most visitors dash by car from Chepstow to Tintern in ten minutes, view the abbey ruins and belt into the gift shops and pubs that line the road through the village. But a little sauntering pays a lot of dividends in the Wye Valley.

You can enjoy a good day's walk up the whole 18-mile (29-km) length of the valley from Chepstow to Monmouth, seeing only other walkers and hearing little but bird-song and river rush, by following the opening section of the Offa's Dyke Path up the almost roadless east bank of the Wye. Even if you decide to take the car – and that means following the A466 up the west bank and through all the tourist honeypots – you can still get away from the crowds by side-tracking for a very short distance. Even popular viewpoints like Wyndcliff (signposted on the bend of the A466 just beyond St Arvans) are entirely free of crowds outside the very height of the summer season. This great limestone cliff towers 800 feet (244 m) to the viewing platform called the Eagle's Nest, the high spot of a round walk laid out at the peak of the Romantic movement. The view from here stretches for many miles over the treetops, its focal point the great, shining bend of the Wye round Lancaut promontory in the foreground below. In 1828 steps were built in the cliff face – 365 of them – by which you can still descend to the river bank down a zig-zag path overhung with gloomy Victorian evergreens and light, naturally seeded beech and rowan.

Tintern Abbey, 5 miles (8 km) upstream of Chepstow, stands superbly between road and river, always a sight to make you catch your breath and smile with pleasure, no matter how many times you have seen it. The abbey was founded by the Cistercian order in 1131, though hardly anything remains of the original building, which was greatly enlarged in the thirteenth and fourteenth centuries. Time and vandals have done remarkably little damage to the church since it lost its monks and its lead roof in 1536. Pillars, arches and walls all soar like a stone forest, but Tintern's glory is its great windows, east, west and south. The east window, 64 feet (19½ m) tall, retains the top section of its stone tracery and looks across the Wye to the woods and slopes beyond, a celestial view both for medieval monks and twentieth-century visitors. Something about a great window, devoid of glass but with its tracery intact, stirs the heart and imagination as no wall or doorway ever does: Tintern's in particular. Perhaps it's the way each window catches a lovely view and holds it suspended like a picture.

Tintern village, straggling along the A466, might have sprung into being entirely for the benefit of its visitors, judged by the way it looks today. But for centuries the Wye Valley was a hive of industry, with wireworks, ironworks, forges, paper mills and tin plate manufactories. There were coal pits and iron mines in the Forest of Dean just across the river, plenty of water power from streams falling down the steep side valleys to join the Wye, and the river itself as a transport route. Tintern's own wireworks were set up only thirty years after the monks had left, the first such works in Britain to be powered by water. The works switched over to producing tin plate in the 1880s, and flickered out of life altogether at the turn of the century. They had brought employment, life and some prosperity to the little Wyeside village, thudding and clashing a measure of reality into the romantic vision of all those Georgian and Victorian tourists.

'All description must fall short of its awful grandeur', wrote John Byng on visiting Tintern Abbey (ABOVE) in 1781, when he found so much of the stonework such as the entrance portal (LEFT), 'in the highest state of preservation a ruin can be in'. Its beautiful setting among the woods and above the River Wye has made Tintern Abbey, ever since the eighteenth century, one of the principal sights to be enjoyed by the Border traveller.

The remains of the industry lie along the side valley of the Angidy Brook, up which a lane marked 'Raglan' climbs from the centre of Tintern. There is nothing left of the wireworks themselves, but about a mile (1½ km) up the valley the little brook is crossed by a succession of old dams and sluices, while on the right of the road the arches and walls of the Angidy Ironworks furnace lie under the trees, neatly excavated and displayed. Old cottages stand deep in the dell by the brook, backed by the tree-covered slopes of the valley side, shaded from the sun for all but a couple of hours a day. Most mark the site of one of the long-forgotten one- or two-man operations – blast furnace, forge or mill – that made this now silent valley an industrial centre for so long. After exploring the valley, stop off at the Cherry Tree Inn just before you reach the A466 in Tintern again. This little pub, a first-floor room up a flight of worn stone steps on the right of the road, is an unpretentious place, neat and clean, where decent beer is fetched by the landlord from barrels in the back room, where there is no piped music, no row and no intrusion. Visitors to Tintern jam-pack the pubs along the main road, but the quiet side road and its modest little inn stay – for some inexplicable but blessed reason – out of their ken.

Another excellent inn just off the beaten track, serving food as well, is the Brockweir Inn. Brockweir lies across the Wye, huddled on the east bank around the head of its bridge, in an attractive tangle of lanes. There were many inns and cider houses here when Brockweir was a busy centre of river activity. Above the village the narrowing gorge squeezes the Wye into a thinner course, and a series of weirs blocks the route north. So goods coming up from the Severn by ship were transferred into flat-bottomed barges that could be pulled up to Monmouth over the weirs by teams of nine or ten men known as 'bow-haulers'. Timber came down from the Forest of Dean to take to the river at Brockweir on its journey to Bristol. The village was a meeting place and exchange point, a lively role from which it has gracefully – and perhaps gratefully – retired. The Malthouse Pottery up the lane from the inn does a few very handsome, simple lines in blue and brown glazes.

Through Llandogo, hanging beautifully above the Wye on hillside and river terraces, goes the A466 to cross the river from Wales into England and curve up to Redbrook. The sheer, craggy limestone sides of the Wye's gorge, that gave such drama to the views between Chepstow and Tintern, are here replaced by the softer, more sloping shapes of red sandstone hills. At Redbrook the Wye has bitten down through the soft sandstone to an enormous depth – so deep a cut, in fact, that the old meander loop abandoned by the river lies 400 feet (120 m) above the Wye's present course. The old loop curves north, east and then south with the B4231 to Newland and beyond, then swings round and runs north-west back to Redbrook – a loop shaped like a butterfly's wing, with the body at Newland. Over the millennia the last portion of the loop has been cut away by streams running down to meet the Wye, and here in the Lower Redbrook Valley are the remains – hard to pick out, except near the roadside site of the old tin plate works – of hammer ponds and furnace ponds of the seventeenth and eighteenth centuries, built to dam water which could be released to power drop-hammers and blow furnace bellows. It makes a lovely walk, curving south up the narrow-sided valley to remote Glyn Farm, a tall old farmhouse standing over a cluttered, old-fashioned farmyard; then north again along the abandoned loop of the river by way of Lodges Farm to where the valley widens into Newland village and the western outskirts of the Forest of Dean.

Writing of the Forest of Dean as an outsider is an almost impossible task. It's like writing of the Scottish islands without knowing any Gaelic. You are either a Forester or you aren't, say the Foresters themselves; and if you aren't you'll never understand the place. The Forest of Dean has always sustained a shifting, self-reliant population. Since before Roman times men have dug and delved, hammered and smelted, chopped and burned, felled and replanted on this plateau full of coal and iron and covered with the biggest concentration of trees on the Welsh Borders. From the early Middle Ages onwards, mining squatters set up house in shacks, caves and old mine-holes, felled virgin areas of the Forest to create patches of open land and took to a life of part-mining, part-grazing and part-poaching. The trees and the industry have gone hand in hand during these many centuries, of course, the one felled to fuel the other. At one time, during the

*The evidence of industrial working to be found throughout the Forest of Dean, such
as this quarry near Coleford, tells the story of many generations of Forest families
winning a living from the minerals beneath the surface.*

Civil War years, the Forest landowner Sir John Winter was felling 100,000 trees a year. At another, during Victorian times, the Forest was stripped nearly bare of its native oaks, to satisfy the demands of shipbuilders and charcoal-burners. But replanting programmes have always seen the trees return as their guardians plan for the future. Coal-mining boomed and slumped in the Forest, as did iron-working, according to the ebb and flow of the tides of history. Road-building cut great swathes through the Forest during the eighteenth century, and opened up hitherto inaccessible areas. The coal industry had a long period of success feeding the Industrial Revolution, and though iron-working went into a trough during the eighteenth century when tree-felling for charcoal was discouraged so as to safeguard timber stocks for the Navy, it revived in the long peace of the post-Waterloo world.

The iron industry of the Forest is now dead, the coal-mining all but gone. But the Foresters themselves remain a tough, independent people, on their guard against the effusive or inquisitive outsider, dry of wit and bloody of mind – very much as Yorkshire folk like to think of themselves, though the Yorkshireman's proudly maintained bluntness of speech turns in the Forest into something more elliptical and self-concealing. Foresters have special privileges: rights of common grazing, for example, and the right of any man of 21 or over born within the Hundred of St Briavels, who has worked in a Forest coal-mine for a year and a day, to apply for a 'gale' or grant of Crown land and mine it himself as a Forest of Dean Freeminer. There are laws peculiar to the Forest, and courts to maintain them, some more ceremonial than effective these days, but all carefully upheld. The Court of Verderers is the best known, an ancient institution set up perhaps as long ago as the reign of King Canute, whose members are charged by the Crown to preserve 'vert and venison'– in other words, all things growing and living in the Forest. In medieval times the Court of Verderers could condemn a serf to death for killing the king's deer; these days, however, the four members elected for life by the Forest freeholders tend to oversee no business more dramatic than a little ritual and a pleasant drink and a chat.

The Forest covers in all some 30,000 acres, or 35 square miles (9000 ha), of ground between Wye and Severn, a great oval central area of trees with smaller offshoots and enclosures all round the edge of the plateau. As a sanctuary for wildlife of all kinds – birds, mammals, reptiles, butterflies, insects, plants and of course trees – its value is beyond assessing. Some of its oaks and holly trees are several hundred years old. Walking on one of the hundreds of Forest footpaths under such trees, whether following a trail laid out by the Forestry Commission or simply striking out away from the road on your own, you can experience in the deep silence a sense of your own insignificance that makes the Forest a humbling and sometimes overwhelming place to be. But thank heaven for that.

Newland (pronounced with the stress on the second syllable: 'New-*land*') is a pretty village – something that can't be said of many Forest villages. Old stone houses and barns stand in a pleasant higgledy-piggledy collection along the main street, grouping round the thirteenth-century All Saints' church into a harmonious triangle of old buildings: the Ostrich Inn opposite the church; the long white block of the almshouses built in 1615 for eight men and eight women, 'pious persons'; and Bell's Grammar School of 1639 west of the church, its stone walls mellowed by the years. Looking over these and over the old cottages of the village to high green slopes of fields and the treetops of the Forest enclosing all, you have a perfect picture of snug contentment. Nothing is out of place, nothing is unsightly. Newland seems a privileged place, as indeed it is and was. In its name is a clue to its history; the village was created in a clearing in the Forest in about 1219 by Robert de Wakering, a priest. At that time, in the early Middle Ages, the Crown was trying to encourage clearance and agricultural exploitation of Britain's still enormous acreage of original wildwood, and in 1305 endowed the rector of Newland with tithes from any 'assart' or clearing outside the parish. Not surprisingly, Forest clearance spread rather rapidly from the boundaries of Newland parish and the village became a prosperous place. While the wire and tin industries clattered away to the west in Redbrook, the better-heeled folk settled in Newland. It is still prosperous, but that's not to say that Newland is anything like a cosy Home Counties commuter village. In All Saints' church there are many ancient reminders of the traditional dwellers in the Forest. A Forester lies in effigy on top of his tomb, his feet resting on a lop-eared dog, a hunting horn swinging at his belt along with

Several early Georgian houses skirt the churchyard at Newland, together with the seventeenth-century school and almshouses, making the centre of the village one of the prettiest ensembles in the Forest of Dean.

Newland church has a particularly rich collection of monumental effigies. Sir John Joce, who died in 1344, rests his head on a helm carrying an immense, exuberantly carved Saracen's head.

the remnants of a long sword and a complete hunting knife with finger-holes pierced through the handle. He wears a pleated tunic with puffed sleeves, split-sided boots and a hairstyle resembling dreadlocks, combed back and caught in a hairband. This was Jenkin Wyrall, a Forester-of-Fee, who died in 1457. On another slab is incised a simple but very clear outline of an archer in a wide-brimmed hat and Stuart-style beard, with an arrow stuck in his belt. A third slab carries not only a knight and his lady, Robert and Joan Greyndour (Sir Robert looking, indeed, very grey 'n' dour), but between and above them the small but carefully detailed figure of a medieval Forest of Dean miner, who stands on a helm looking skyward for salvation (or perhaps up his mine shaft for daylight), in a close-fitting cap, with a wooden coal tram or hod on his back, a pick in his hand and a candlestick shaped like an old-fashioned tobacco-pipe clenched in his downturned mouth. Robert de Wakering, priest and founder of the village, lies in effigy in the church, too; the sculptor evidently tried to capture a good likeness of de Wakering, giving him a long jaw and firm mouth set in a thin face. These are all wonderful records in stone and brass, fine works of art in their own right, investing the handsome church with a sense of the continuity of idiosyncratic Forest life. The 'Cathedral of the Forest', as it is known locally, is splendidly wide, tall and full of light, obviously built for a place of some importance. But ordinary Forest industries and their workers were not forgotten. At the turn of the fifteenth century a chapel was founded on the north side of the chancel, to support a priest with a roving job. His task was to say 'Morrow Mass' or early morning mass twice a week for the local miners before they began their long and dangerous day underground.

The B4226 bisects the Forest, from Coleford on the western edge to Cinderford on the east, and these two places will give you in their different ways a very fair idea of the flavour of Forest towns. There is nothing in any way smart or fashionable about them; they are working places with working populations, rooted as their names suggest in the coal and the iron ore cinders of Forest industry. Coleford has the splendid Forest Book Shop in St John's Street, just below the clock tower in the former market place, an establishment run with friendly efficiency by Douglas McLean, whose town walkabout booklet will show you all the best hidden corners of Coleford. Mushet Place, on the long hill sloping into the town from the south, is named after David and Robert Mushet, father and son, who were pioneers in the manufacture of cast steel. On the corner is a rusty old wall plaque recording Robert Mushet's contribution to perfecting the Bessemer process of steel-making in 1856, and his discovery twelve years later of self-hardening steel. The Mushets lived at Forest House just below, now a small hotel. By turning left at the clock tower at the bottom of the hill and walking out of town along Newland Street you can find on the right hand side of the road the remains of one of the enormous blast furnaces that smelted Coleford's iron ore – great stone walls, arches and ramps set under the hillside. There are some fine large chapels in the town, built for the thousands of industrial workers of Victorian Coleford; notably the Baptist chapel of 1850 at the top of Newland Street, with its twin towers under pointed witch-hat roofs and its enormously tall romanesque windows, and the sadly dilapidated Independent Congregational chapel of 1842 glowering below the triumphal red bulk of the Church of England edifice.

There are some old and handsome hotels and other buildings to be spotted round Coleford's town centre, but at Cinderford on the opposite side of the Forest the eye has to content itself with the splendid views from the town's hilltop position. From the nineteenth century Cinderford grew on coal and iron, a tough and arid-looking settlement of stone and slate with no frills or fancies to it. Side lanes lead off among run-down shops and plain workers' terraces to tremendous views over the Forest, stretching away in dark and light waves to the western horizon. The Baptists were a force to be reckoned with in Victorian Cinderford, holding an annual August Bank Holiday Treat with processions, brass bands and a heroic tea for all comers. Their giant chapel of 1860, by contrast, stands dourly on the side of the town ridge, drab and looming, an uncompromising manufactory of saved souls.

Half-way between Coleford and Cinderford, right in the centre of the Forest, stands the Speech House, built in 1680 to house the Court of Verderers. The court still holds its meetings here in the great dining room, and in another chamber the Freeminers of the Forest also congregate in due season. The Baptists of Cinderford had their holy rout in August, but here among the trees the miners held more worldly celebrations each July at their own Demonstration, with a grand fair, speeches, bands, sideshows and prodigious drinking. These days the Speech House is an extremely comfortable and friendly hotel, where in the bar the senior citizens of the Forest sit in a long line of chairs along the wall to put the world to rights in their rich, burring Gloucestershire accents with a hint of Welsh and a touch of something else peculiar to the Forest. A network of walks spreads in all directions from the Speech House, winding off under the trees and down into hidden valleys: the Bixslade Forest Walk, for example, through oaks and sweet chestnuts planted in Napoleonic times, and by old quarries and coal-mines; or the trail through the Cannop Valley Nature Reserve along forest tracks and old tramways and railways around a string of bird-haunted streams and ponds.

One of the best ways to catch a quick insight into Forest life and traditions is to seek out one of the small handful of coal-mines still in operation, chat to the miners and see if you can get yourself invited to go down the mine. The mine in Bream Copse operated by Donald Johns and Gilbert Kear is a typical Forest pit. Donald and Gilbert between them have put in almost a century of work in tiny shoe-string coal-mines in various parts of the Forest of Dean. Foresters born and bred, they have known no other work and would not take another occupation for any money. They sell their coal – maybe ten tons a day – to British Coal, who send it on to the power station at Newport. There's little money in the Bream Copse mine – that's not why Donald and Gilbert keep at it, day after day. They simply enjoy the work, the freedom from regulations and restrictions, and the exercising of their immemorial right as Freeminers to win their modest living in their own way and at their own pace.

The mouth of the mine is a square black hole framed with timbers into which a line of rails tips and vanishes. The entrance slopes steeply down, floored with slippery clay or 'clod' as Gilbert calls it. About 20 yards (18 m) underground the shaft turns at right angles into a roadway 4 feet (1 m) high, a curving tunnel just wide enough to take either Gilbert or Donald as, bent double, they push the little 'dram' or coal truck in front of them to the coal face. The only light comes from the helmet lamp of whichever of the partners is in the mine. The floor where the rails run is of damp earth, and the sides are shored up with pit props of pine wood rammed in place by the two men as they drive their way forward week by week.

At the coal face, 100 yards (90 m) along the roadway, solid walls of coal glint between the pit props. Here the coal, loosened from the face earlier in the day by an explosive shot, is shovelled from a sitting position over the shoulder into the dram. Then the heavy dram is pushed back along the rails to the bottom of the incline and attached to a cable. The outside partner, waiting above for a ring on the home-made bell system, sets the winch going and draws the laden dram slowly up out of the mine.

There are very few mines like this still operating in the Forest, three or four, perhaps, all of them worked by elderly men. The Freeminers still meet twice a year, but they have no real power in the modern coal industry, though on occasion they unite to defeat or sidestep what they see as unnecessarily fussy planning regulations. The youngsters, Donald Johns says, are not interested in hard labour for scant reward. The Forest and all it stands for, he thinks, is being bred out of the local children.

The low-lying country that sweeps away from the eastern edge of the Forest of Dean to meet the broad curves of the River Severn does not really fall inside the boundaries of the Welsh Borders, wide though I have drawn them. This area, like the Forest, is sufficient unto itself, a landscape held together more by the river than by any political, historical or emotive Border influence. The people who live here would probably not consider themselves Borderers at all. The following excursion, therefore, is by way of being a sidetrack among villages and hamlets with their own distinctive Severnside atmosphere a little removed from the main flow of this tour.

The A4151 runs east from Cinderford to meet the A48 and skirt the river at Westbury-on-Severn, where Westbury Court Garden, a beautiful formal Dutch water garden laid out between 1696 and 1705, has recently been restored by the National Trust. A wonderful feeling of calm and order emanates from the square-cut hedges, the rectangular pools of water, the lounging statues and the elegant brick summerhouse. All this was a neglected shambles until the National Trust took it in hand in the early 1970s. The grounds contain a tall and stately tulip tree, and an ilex whose trunk has been fantastically knobbled by three or four centuries of growth.

Near the water garden stands the church, whose detached spire glows with 60,000 tiny, silver-grey wooden shingles. In May 1644 a force of Royalists was quartered in Westbury Court and in the church itself. A troop of Roundhead soldiers took over the tower, and stood on stools and ladders to fire out of its windows into the church. They drove out the Royalists and then stormed the house, killing twenty of their opponents and capturing eighty without losing a single man themselves. Another story tells of a Spanish spy sent to the district just before the launching of the Armada with orders to set fire to the Forest of Dean. He was hiding in Westbury tower one Sunday morning when the bells suddenly began to ring, knocking him from his perch to his death.

Opposite the church a footpath leads down Bell Lane beside the Red Lion Inn, across stiles and over the fields, to reach an old quay on a broad bend of the Severn. The river, about half a mile (1 km) wide, curves majestically under the red and white strata of Garden Cliff. Though there are villages in view, they are diminished by distance to little smudges on a big canvas of grass, trees and water. This is a lonely and beautiful spot.

A winding lane runs north through Oakle Street, Bulley and Tibberton, small settlements in wide valleys with the long line of the Cotswold hills lying far away in the east. Ancient orchards stand behind the smallholdings that put out fruit stalls beside the road in summer. The farms spatter their mud generously across the road in this damp land of meadows and drainage ditches lined with pollarded willows. At Hartpury the view holds all the elements of a Constable painting – the old brick-built water mill across the meadows, complete with its water-wheel, the church tower peeping up above the trees, the mellow stone roof of the fourteenth-century tithe barn. Massively buttressed, the barn stands 160 feet (49 m) long and nearly 40 feet (12 m) wide. Inside the building light pours in dusty shafts through the slit windows, above which hangs a tremendous medieval timber roof where pigeons coo and flutter. Across the lane stand the little Norman church and the fifteenth-century Court House, now a farmhouse where many hundred years' building styles in stone and brick are comfortably jumbled together.

At Ashleworth you meet the River Severn again, having cut a chord by road across the looping, 10-mile (16-km) arc it makes round Gloucester. The narrow minor road runs north-east towards Tewkesbury along the river valley, throwing off side lanes down to lonely pubs and deserted quays on the Severn's west bank, reminders of days past when the river was more important than any road as a through route for goods. At the

*The broad and mighty river flows beneath the striped red and white cliffs
at Westbury-on Severn, their feet exposed at low tide to show off their
impressive scale.*

bottom of the side turning to Ashleworth Quay stands another lovely grouping of medieval stone buildings – tithe barn, manor house and church clustered together on the brink of the river.

This is flood country, where in spring the Severn rises to pour over its rim and across the low-lying land. The two elderly Jelf sisters who run the Boat Inn at Ashleworth Quay calmly continue pulling pints, standing in rubber boots in water almost up to their knees, for any customers loyal or thirsty enough to venture by boat or by wading to the marooned pub on the river bank. When the floods go down they mop up philosophically and get on with their lives. Jelfs have been at Ashleworth for at least 600 years. King Charles II (as he became in 1660), in flight from the Battle of Worcester, granted a Jelf ancestor the right to run a ferry across the Severn in return for a lift over in his boat – a right only relinquished in recent years. The Boat Inn makes no concessions to modern

The huge 125-feet-long tithe barn at Ashleworth built at the end of the fifteenth century, and the earlier great barn at nearby Hartpury, are testimony to the medieval wealth of this stretch of the Severn Valley.

tastes. There is no piped music, no fruit machine or smart menu. The beer is drawn from a barrel in a dark back scullery. If there is enough cheese in the larder the Jelfs may cut you a sandwich to go with your beer and pickled egg. Conversation rumbles along among the old sofas and stuffed armchairs – the floods, the weather, local gossip.

Rejoining the minor road at the top of the lane, you meander on between the meadows and the willows, through Tirley and Chaceley with their farms and orchards. In St Michael's church at Tirley there is a puzzle – piscina and holy water stoup are down almost at floor level, and the door arches seem unnaturally low and out of proportion. The solution lies in the river: the church floor had to be raised to cope with the Severn flooding. St John the Baptist's at Chaceley is rich in Norman and fourteenth-century stone carving and woodwork. The keystone of the chevroned Norman chancel arch is carved with a bulging devil's face that could well be Saxon artistry.

At Chaceley Stock, as at Ashleworth Quay, you will find an old river quay and a pub down a long side track. The bright and popular Yew Tree Inn at Chaceley Stock sees fifty customers to every one that visits the Jelfs at Ashleworth Quay. But the February floods plunge both pubs impartially into a watery isolation.

Above Chaceley the long road bends through Forthampton Green – black-and-white, thatched and pretty medieval houses and farms, cluttered farmyards, orchards and cottage gardens, gabled almshouses and a low-ceilinged church whose south doorway shows a slant-eyed, pagan-looking king, half lion and half man, with leopard-like companions. From the churchyard there is a wide view to the towers of Tewkesbury Abbey and the long Severn Valley south towards Chaceley and east to the Cotswolds. Continue up the road to join the M50 motorway just north of Tewkesbury. Here, turning west towards Ross-on-Wye and Border country, our Severn side track ends.

The motorway sweeps you south-west in a trice, from the Severn back to the Wye. The Wye curls at the feet of Ross-on-Wye in a loop known as Horseshoe Bend. The M50 meets the A449, and immediately Ross is signposted on the left. But carry a little further along the A449, turning off into the town on the A40 for the sake of the grand view, from the bridge over the Wye, of the houses and town walls of Ross stepping up the flank of their sandstone bluff to the 205-foot (62-m) spire of St Mary's church. It all looks very historic; but in fact those 'medieval' town walls were built in the 1830s when Ross was trying to forge a new prosperity for itself as a holiday and resort town. There is an excellent 'Ross-on-Wye Walkabout' leaflet, available from the town's bookshops and tourist office, which will take you round the sloping streets that centre on the long, red sandstone Market House; built in about 1670, it stands on its pillars where Broad Street meets High Street. You will find many a market hall in the town centres of the Welsh Borders, and that of Ross is a good example – solid, dominating the streets, with a rag-bag market inside the open ground floor selling everything from underwear to plant seeds, all cheap, all cheerful.

Opposite the Market House is the half-timbered house which was once the home of John Kyrle, the celebrated 'Man of Ross'. Kyrle stares out from a wall medallion in a full, curly wig. He died in 1724, aged 88, in the happy position of a philanthropist who had seen the fruits of his generosity flourishing on his own home patch. No man did more for his town, and few have been better remembered. Everyone in Ross-on-Wye knows of the Man of Ross, who inherited £500 a year in his twenties, and settled down in Ross to spend the lot on his fellow men. When he died, John Kyrle neither owned nor owed a penny.

The Severn-side towns and villages are continually vigilant against the danger of flooding, which happens with insistent regularity. The swollen river again places the parish church at Tirley (ABOVE) in jeopardy as it bursts its banks, and threatens the Abbey Mill and the sandbagged quayside houses at Tewkesbury (LEFT) a few miles upstream.

Peering out through the red sandstone pillars of Ross-on Wye's market hall (ABOVE), built soon after Charles II was restored to the throne, the view of the half-timbered frontages of the houses is typical of towns on the border. Opposite stands the former home of John Kyrle, the 'Man of Ross', who planted some of the trees in the pretty churchyard of St Mary's (RIGHT).

Ross-on-Wye had benefited, though: there were schools for its children; a water supply and public garden for all its citizens; a causeway over the meadows to bring the people of Ross safely to the bridge when the Wye was in flood; food and clothing for the poor; medicine for the sick; encouragement, advice and money for those wanting to get started in business. Behind his house, on a raised piece of ground behind high sandstone walls, stands the formal garden and the summerhouse that he built. I gained entry to this private paradise through an upper window at the rear of the premises of Rowberry & Co. in High Street, dropping down into a wilderness of overgrown grass and tangled trees in which were still laid out the skeletons of John Kyrle's hedged knot garden, bowling green and walkways through arched tunnels. The weather-beaten, crumbling summerhouse stood against the boundary wall, ruinous and tottering. In front of its door I found the mosaic of a white swan, half-sunk in the ground, which Kyrle had had made in another philanthropic gesture. The pieces of the mosaic are not of stone; they are hundreds of horses' teeth, retrieved at so much a tooth by poor townspeople from the meadows near Wilton Bridge on the western outskirts of Ross where a Civil War skirmish had been fought out. The garden was soon to be restored by the owner of Rowberry & Co., so I was told; he was planning to refurbish the summerhouse and live there himself. There may soon be no more exploratory leaps through that back window.

The Man of Ross devoted a large part of his fortune to the upkeep of St Mary's church; he rebuilt its spire and donated a new tenor bell, at whose casting he threw his own silver tankard into the molten metal. You can reach St Mary's in a short walk up Church Street. Beside the churchyard path stands a stone cross whose inscription records in a few stark words the horror of a plague outbreak in Ross:

An° Dom¹ 1637
Burials 315
Libera nos Domine

The church contains a lovely east window with stained-glass lights of 1430 showing various upward-looking saints and a little kneeling figure of Bishop Spofford (who had the window made), offering his tiny red heart to a baby Virgin Mary sitting on her mother's knee. There are some splendid marble babes, skulls, noble warriors and sorrowing widows among the monuments to the Rudhall family, but only a modest plaque and grave slab to the Man of Ross. His memory is kept green – literally – by the Virginia creepers that climb from a stone trough up the inside of the east window in the north aisle. They are replacements for the elm suckers that pushed their way under and into the church from the trees planted in the churchyard by John Kyrle. The public gardens he gave to the town – The Prospect – lie just beyond the church at the edge of the river cliff, giving a memorable view down over Horseshoe Bend, enclosing its single great field, north and west to the Welsh hills.

From Ross-on-Wye the B4228 and the B4229 take you south and west across the Wye to another splendid Border fortification, the great red block of Goodrich Castle, which rises from the jagged slab of sandstone on which it is founded, its square moat hacked out of the same stone. The twelfth-century keep and thirteenth-century walls, though battered by the famous 200-pounder cannon 'Roaring Meg' in the Civil War, and partly pulled down when captured, still look every inch a medieval castle, from whose ramparts a trumpet might sound at any moment. This is the place to let children's legs and imaginations run free. There are vantage points at various heights in the walls – all safely fenced off – looking out over the surrounding countryside and the snaking Wye; and the grimmest and darkest of ill-lit dungeons entered by a needle's-eye of a doorway under the keep.

For a final high prospect over the country of the River Wye, though, one has to give pride of place to the best-known viewpoint – the rearing rock of Symond's Yat, climbing from a meander of the river that takes 4 miles ($6\frac{1}{2}$ km) to return to within 500 yards (450 m) of where it started. There is only one road into and out of the meander; it leaves the B4229 just south of Goodrich and crosses the Wye, to bisect a vast flat cornfield that could be in Suffolk or Norfolk were it not for the hills that enclose it. A path leaves the car park just below the cliff face on the neck of the river loop, and climbs to the flat viewing platform 500 feet (150 m) up. You look down over the treetops on to the sloping back of Huntsman Hill and the slow-flowing Wye looping far below. This northward view is at its best in autumn, when the whole of Huntsman Hill glows and blazes with gold, red and dusky green. Little white houses, built in picturesque tiers by Victorian scenery-fanatics, peep from the river cliff. To the east is the long, bracken-smothered back of Coppet Hill, and to the south a great swathe of the Forest of Dean, where above the river rise the tall limestone cliffs where peregrines have been nesting since 1982 after an absence of thirty years. And standing high and handsome in the distance over in the far north-west lie long ridges, beckoning you on into the next tour: the Black Mountains.

One of the best-known beauty spots in the Welsh Borders, the view from Symond's Yat of the River Wye far below as it curves through the flood plain (OPPOSITE) *is matchless.*

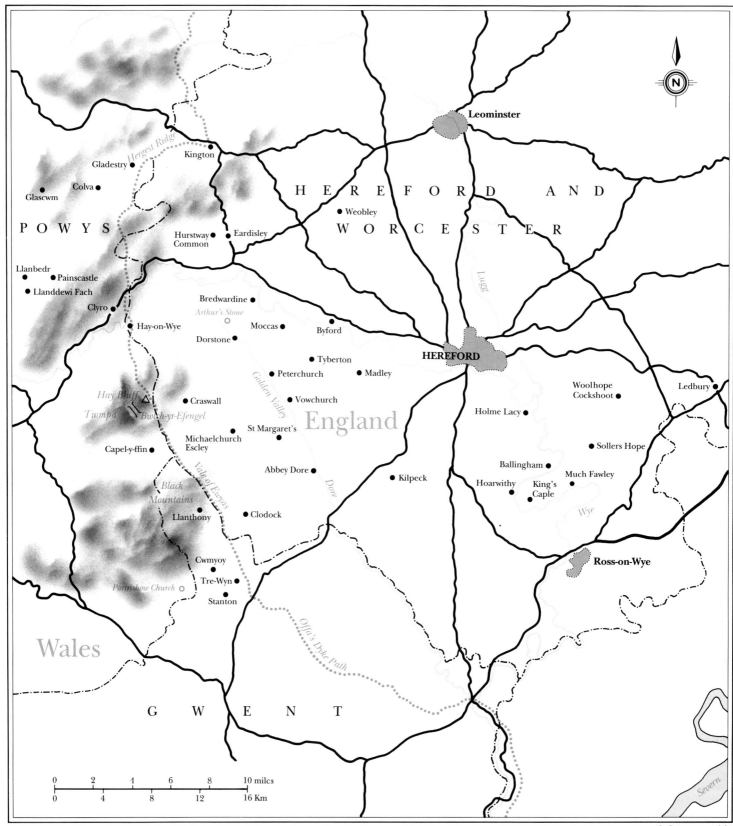

2

Hereford and the
Black Mountains

HEREFORD · LEDBURY · LEOMINSTER · WEOBLEY · HERGEST RIDGE
CLYRO · HAY-ON-WYE · BLACK MOUNTAINS · LLANTHONY · PARTRISHOW
KILPECK · THE GOLDEN VALLEY

I f you want to get the best out of a wander around the city of Hereford, it's not necessarily a good idea to start with the cathedral. So rich are the treasures both outside and inside that beautiful sandstone heart of the city that you are likely to find them milling around in your head all day, obscuring humbler — but no less fascinating — delights of Hereford's compact medieval streets. Let the cathedral be a glorious finale to this leisurely ramble, and ease yourself by slow degrees into the swirling river of Borders history that has washed through Hereford for the best part of 2000 years.

Standing squarely on one of the few lowland routes between England and Wales, its southern outskirts on a ford across the wide River Wye, Hereford was always in the front line of warfare. The Saxons named it 'War Ford' and King Offa of Mercia walled it in against the Welsh. Well before the Norman Conquest there was a Norman castle here, built by Count Ralph of Normandy who had been invited over by his uncle Edward the Confessor (1042–66) to deal with the insurgent Welsh and the upsurgent local Saxon lords. The Welsh burned the wooden castle in 1055, almost as soon as it was finished, but within a dozen years a new one of stone was rising above the Wye. What a turbulent, up-and-down story then followed: burnings, sackings, punitive raids sallying out against the Welsh; attacks during King Stephen's wars with Matilda; Henry III and his son, the future Edward I, prisoners in the castle; executions of Welsh chieftains in the city centre. There was a medieval heyday as a prosperous market town when all the southern cattle-droving roads seemed to lead to Hereford. During the Civil War, an army of Scots laid siege to the city for a month without taking it; but it fell in a few hours to Colonel John Birch, the holy Roundhead terror. Decline and depression followed, until eighteenth-century gentry turned Hereford into a fashionable winter resort; then came a shake-up of the city's antiquated sewerage and water supply, the arrival of the railway in the 1850s and a measure of stability at long last. By the late nineteenth century, Hereford had settled down to its role as administrative, social and industrial centre of a countryside no longer riven by war and want.

From the tree-lined, peaceful cathedral green make your way down Quarry Street just outside the east gates of the green. Here is a fine collection of the handsome red-brick houses built by those Georgian squires who preferred to winter in the warmth and muted bustle of the little city, away from the chilly stone halls and manors of their Herefordshire estates. The well-proportioned houses look out over their walled plots on to Redcliffe Gardens, where squats a modernistic bandstand painted a sickly green, splendidly out of place among its mellow neighbours. Just beyond is the open space of Castle Green, once enclosed by the bailey of the entirely vanished Hereford Castle. The castle motte, just above Redcliffe Gardens, was flattened during the course of eighteenth-century improvements to the city, and in 1809 the citizens of Hereford erected a column in the centre of Castle Green in memory of the 'Gallant Hero' Lord Nelson and his 'career of unexampled glory'. Unfortunately the money ran out just before the memorial was finished, so an inexpensive urn stands on top in place of the intended statue of the hero. From the pathway along the outer edge of the Green there is a good view down to the graceful cast-iron Victoria Footbridge. The bridge was built across the Wye just after Queen Victoria's Diamond Jubilee (1897) to give the people of Hereford easy access to their favourite strolling grounds in the Bishop's Meadow on the south bank of the river.

Following the path back round the western side of Castle Green and by the end of the long duck pool (once part of the castle moat), you reach broad St Owen Street in the city centre by way of St Ethelbert Street. Along on the right, at the point where St Owen's Gate pierced the old city walls of Hereford, the Barrels offers you a strong tang of the highly idiosyncratic flavour of a Hereford pub. Scruffy dogs wander in and out among the regulars at the bar. The walls carry ancient advertisements for long-deceased brands of tobacco, and the notice board rustles with layers of handbills – outings, darts matches, the Christmas Club. The seats of the well-worn settles in the bar have been shaped so exactly by generations of Hereford bottoms that they slide you gently backwards into the most comfortable possible position. Old men sit in pairs at the tables, swearing quietly over their fruitless betting slips. Out in the stables behind the pub the Wye Valley Brewery, fragrant with malt and hops smells, makes a few barrels every week of its pale gold, sweet-tasting Hereford Pale Ale. 'I'm a publican by economic necessity', the landlord of the Barrels told me as he showed me round the tiny brewery. 'But I'm a brewer here in my heart.' Barrels regulars become cider drinkers in their hearts after the age of fifty – not clear cider from commercial companies, but stuff that clouds both glass and judgement.

St Owen Street takes you west past the florid Edwardian turrets and terracotta curlicues of the Town Hall, towards St Peter's church, founded in 1074. The Marcher Lord Walter de Lacy, inspecting the building of the church in 1085, leaned too far over the battlements and fell to his death in the street below. Unfortunately the church is kept

Throughout the tightly-built centre of Hereford there are glimpses of the great, square crossing tower of Hereford Cathedral (OPPOSITE), built in pink-grey sandstone, with the ancient streets packed close around.

locked. The Old House, however, just along the street in the central area of the city called High Town, is usually open and occasionally free of entry. This striking old half-timbered house, built in 1621, is rightly seen by the city as one of its best focal points. Now a brick-paved pedestrian precinct, this end of High Town was until the early nineteenth century a maze of narrow streets, one of those fetid medieval centres of butchery that went under the generic name of The Shambles. Probably built for a master butcher, the Old House is now a museum of Herefordshire life in Stuart times, full to the eaves with dark, heavy, seventeenth-century furniture, kitchen equipment and carved fireplaces. I particularly liked the wall-paintings in the house, some in their original place and others brought from houses in and around Hereford: a peasant on the kitchen wall, stolidly digging with a triangular spade; saints staring over celestial city walls; and upstairs in the living room a demurely smiling, blond-haired Urania, the Muse of Astronomers, about to deal herself a nasty jab with a sharp pair of dividers. On the top floor of the house there are dark little bedrooms on creaky floors, from where latticed windows look down on a crowded street. Above a fireplace here hangs a wooden panel

The exuberantly carved decoration on the entrance to the early Stuart Old House provides access to Hereford's museum of seventeenth-century life, in which the decorations of the building itself are among the prime exhibits.

entitled 'The Law Suit'. Two men are disputing the ownership of a cow, one in breeches and a wide-brimmed hat pulling her tail, his opponent yanking at the horns while his fallen hat lies in the mud. Between them sits a lawyer in a curly wig, calmly milking the cow – and, by inference, the two litigants. Some things haven't changed since the Old House was built.

A little further along High Town is the Butter Market, opened in 1860, a covered market where country Herefordshire comes to town. This is a real market, a jostling, loud-mouthed place of tightly packed stalls where most items are cheap and few are non-negotiable. You need a will of iron to emerge from Hereford's Butter Market with your money still in your pocket. The stalls are crammed with handbags, shoes, electrical goods, plants, sweets, cheese, bread, toys and flowers – and butter. Kington Farm Produce has a stall literally piled with eggs. D. J. Benjamin & Sons display glistening slabs of cod, herring and flatfish – 'Straight from the Sea'. On the benches of Gemma's Handy Café flop the exhausted market-goers, tired out from haggling and chaffing the stall-holders, sipping cups of tea and groaning with laughter over their purchases.

You leave the Butter Market through a tiled passageway with your ears ringing, to emerge in Widemarsh Street opposite Black's dress shop. In a former incarnation, Black's was the Lord Mayor's mansion house. At some more recent date it became a pork butcher's, witness the tiled picture in its doorway of contentedly smiling pigs chewing rushes by a stream.

From Black's, walking north along Widemarsh Street, you pass the end of Maylord Street on the right, where on the wall of a shabby, forlorn old building hangs an ancient blue plaque (almost venerable enough to qualify for a blue plaque itself) recording the site of the birthplace of the actor-manager David Garrick. Garrick, the darling of Georgian London's theatre-goers, was born in an inn here in 1717. Though his birthplace is so neglected, Hereford's most celebrated theatrical son has had his name perpetuated in the glaring red council offices – Garrick House – where Widemarsh Street meets the rushing dual carriageway of Newmarket Street. Once across this dangerous junction it's a short walk up to a neat little rose garden on the right. In the centre stand the ruined walls of the cloisters of Hereford's Black Friars' Priory, built in 1332 and largely destroyed two hundred years later during Henry VIII's frenzied campaign against the monasteries. The preaching cross near the ruins, of roughly the same date as the priory, has somehow remained intact – a unique survival. Over the hedge is the long, low range of the Coningsby Hospital. Founded in 1614 by Sir Thomas Coningsby, who was using the half-ruined buildings of the priory as his own house, the hospital still shelters elderly servicemen, most of them veterans of the two World Wars.

Walking back down Widemarsh Street, take the time to peer through the palings of fences and behind the advertisement hoardings. Here before re-entering the old-fashioned charm of High Town you can catch a different slant on Hereford's history – crazily sagging, twisted and semi-derelict backyard sheds and workshops, one-man factories which once fed the prosperity of the city. Back in High Town, All Saints' church points a crooked spire over the streets. The tower that underpins the spire was itself built over a ditch and when the spire was added to the tower in the fourteenth century the extra weight caused the tower to subside into the hollow, twisting the new spire out of line. Inside the church, as tall and bare as a barn, are splendid misericords contemporary with the spire, hidden under the tip-up seats of the choir. They include a

The ruins of the fourteenth-century house of the Order of St John of Jerusalem were
converted into Coningsby Hospital in 1614 by Sir Thomas Coningsby, whose own
house, in the old Dominican friary buildings, lay behind.

devil with a Fu Manchu moustache grimacing between his legs, fighting dragons and two
wild, pagan faces leering out of foliage.

Turn left from the church into High Town and right down narrow Capuchin Lane
(known to former generations of Herefordians as 'Cabbage Lane') which leads to Church
Street and its craft workshops in Capuchin Yard. At the end of the street rears the
cathedral, but before entering it spare a few minutes to enjoy the houses and lanes
around the green. The citizens of Hereford hurry by, heads down, past the 700-year-old
cathedral barn, and the house along a walled lane on the east where Alfred Watkins,
author of a cranky and half-convincing book on leylines and mysterious forces, *The Old
Straight Track*, came in 1920 to spend the last fifteen years of his long life.

Muted pink-grey light softens the interior of Hereford cathedral, reflecting off
massive Norman piers and chevron-cut round arches of faded sandstone. Norman
heaviness in the twelfth-century nave rises to Norman lightness – but still solid enough –
in the second and third storeys of the choir. Later craftsmen have their moments of glory

The early twentieth-century west end of Hereford cathedral – which replaced the front put up after the great west tower collapsed in 1786 – provides few clues to the twelfth- and thirteenth-century glories of the interior.

in the Lady Chapel and its underlying crypt on the east end of the building (Early English, of about 1220); the fourteenth-century stalls of the choir with their misericords that feature dragons, angels and a goose defiantly pecking the fox that has her by the neck; Bishop Stanbury's Chantry, wonderfully fan-vaulted in gothic exuberance of the late 1400s. The monuments, too, would by themselves merit a visit : the painted Tudor effigies of Alexander Denton and his wife, their baby strapped in swaddling bands and cuddled in the folds of its mother's red cloak; Sir Peter de Grandisson (1358) by a carver of the Herefordshire School of Sculpture, a lively and finely detailed effigy with a dog looking up from his position under Sir Peter's mailed feet, tongue out and lop ears cocked, still hoping to hear his master's voice again. The late thirteenth-century tomb of St Thomas of Hereford (1218–82), a bishop whose remains caused miraculous healings, shows Knights Templar beating their breasts and hanging their heads in sorrow – or perhaps in disbelief at the apparition that floats over the tomb, a modern metal creation by David Watkins in pink, purple and silver, shaped like a car luggage rack.

The mighty Norman pillars in the nave of Hereford cathedral (ABOVE), each some 7 feet in diameter, carry the upper parts which were rebuilt by James Wyatt in 1788 after the collapse of the west tower. In the nave the alabaster effigy of Sir Richard Pembridge, who lies with his mailed head resting upon an exquisitely carved helmet (RIGHT), survived both the disaster and the restorer's attentions.

Two of the cathedral's chief treasures are not on display in the main body of the church. To see the Chained Library of 1444 books, you have to climb a spiral stair in the north wall of the church. This is the biggest and by far the best chained library in the world, the books attached to long chains so that they can be taken from the shelves and read at the benches between the bookcases, but not removed further. There are many unique manuscripts in this upper room. They include a snippet from a seventh-century St Matthew's Gospel, and all four Gospels from a century later, as well as marvellously illustrated breviaries, Books of Hours, homilies and other devotional works. The finest workmanship on display is in the fourteenth-century Decretals of Gratian, a compilation of church law largely unintelligible to the layman – but what exquisite beauty of line, colour and shading in the gilded miniature and the red and blue capital letters at which the book lies open. The brownish ink was probably made of walnut juice mixed with gum, and the colours themselves of natural dyes, laid on to the wafer-thin animal-skin page with brushes of animal hair – mouse whiskers for certain of the finest details. How much monkish eyesight that book consumed during its creation I don't like to think.

The name of the artist or artists who worked on the Decretals of Gratian may be unknown to us, but at least we can be fairly sure of the name of the creator of Hereford cathedral's other great treasure, now on display in the crypt under the Lady Chapel. Richard de Bello must have had tremendous fun when he drew and coloured his big circular Mappa Mundi ('map of the world') in 1289. Putting Jerusalem in the centre, and squashing the British Isles in a sleeping-dog shape into the corner, De Bello jammed together the known and the unknown world, biblical events and mythological events, established facts and wild conjectures, to leave for posterity a wonderfully detailed picture of how an educated man viewed the world at the end of the thirteenth century. It's his vigorous, humorous draughtsmanship that makes De Bello's vision so immediately accessible. Jerusalem is a battlemented wheel-like circle, Alexander's camp a forest of pinnacles, the labyrinth of Crete a whirlpool of walls. The Mediterranean Sea is crammed with fish of all kinds, Africa bulges with rhinoceros and unicorn, salamanders and centaurs, men with grotesquely extended lips, men with eyes in their bellies, men with four eyes. A two-tailed ram defecates at the gates of Antioch. A Norwegian on wooden skis wears a woolly hat complete with little bobble on top. The Golden Fleece lies stretched on the shore of the Black Sea. Up in the Hyperbores, or Arctic regions, the land is filled with ice; down in south-east Asia a sciapod, another mythical creation of the medieval mind, shelters under his own corrugated foot. This is the whole pre-exploration world wrapped up in a single parchment circle and delivered to our twentieth-century door. Thank goodness that the Dean and Chapter have been dissuaded by public outcry from their plan to sell the Mappa Mundi for £9 million. News of the scheme hit the headlines in 1989, causing such embarrassment to the cathedral authorities that they had to rethink their intention. Now a new block is to be built to house the cathedral treasures, Chained Library and Mappa Mundi among them.

To the south of the cathedral lie the foundations of the hexagonal Chapter House, broken up for building stone in the eighteenth century, and the cloistered quadrangle of the college of the cathedral's Vicars Choral. The Vicars Choral moved into their newly built college in 1472 as a safety measure; the brigands of the Hereford streets made the journey into the cathedral from quarters outside the precincts far too dangerous. The Bishop's Palace stands beside the college, with narrow Gwynne Street running under its wall down towards the Wye. Here, says a plaque on one of the buildings, Nell Gwynne was born in 1650. She died aged 37, it records, having been the Founder of Chelsea Hospital and mother of the 1st Duke of St Albans. Nothing about oranges, kings or Drury Lane triumphs marks the birthplace of another of Hereford's theatrical celebrities. Turning down Bridge Street, just below, you can take a long look back from one of the passing-bays of the fifteenth-century Wye Bridge, over the dimpled eddies of the river below the arches to the cathedral sailing in stately style over the city. Then it's south and west, into deep Herefordshire country, following the Wye down one of its loveliest and least visited stretches.

It's only about 10 miles (16 km) as the crow flies from Hereford down to Ross-on-Wye, but the river travels at least three times as far as that. In great extravagant loops and wriggles it carves its way through the soft red Herefordshire earth, cutting out a series of river peninsulas on whose narrow necks the villages and hamlets are as good as islanded. There is only a handful of bridges to connect these Wye-encircled places with the opposite bank of the river, and they still keep about them an atmosphere of backwater isolation. The Hereford–Ross railway once strung them together, slicing purposefully across all the river loops; but that rural lifeline has long been cut. With no through roads within 4 or 5 miles (6–8 km) of most of them, the Wye Valley villages south of Hereford are sought out by few tourists. Yet they hold splendid old farmhouses, courts and half-timbered halls, and a succession of remarkable churches. These churches alone repay the winding drive. Meandering here along with the Wye, you are in for a series of unadvertised pleasures.

The landscape of this section of the river takes shape as soon as you turn off the A49 Ross-on-Wye road on to the B4399 and leave the mildly industrial outskirts of Hereford. Ancient brick-and-timber barns appear by the roadside. Duck ponds abound. The river valley stretches out in flat meadows where sheep and red Hereford cattle graze, rising in the distance to the low, thickly wooded ridges that form a generous cradle for the Wye. The countryside rolls gently, its farms and villages set either in the plain or half-way up the hillsides, the churches often well away from the little centres of civilization that withdrew to higher ground to escape the river floods. Holme Lacy's church stands in the Wye's meadows outside the village to the east, full of elaborate marble monuments to the Scudamore family who gained the estate through marriage to the Lacy Marcher Lords. James Scudamore at the east end of the church is particularly lifelike, a young Cavalier in a casual sitting position with long, curly locks, while porky cherubs bear down on him holding a laurel wreath. In the next great bend of the river, Ballingham's church of St Dyfrig also keeps its distance from the village. It stands close together with the dignified seventeenth-century Ballingham Hall, a grouping of isolated church, farm, barns and pond that is characteristic of this area. The dedication is a rare one, confined to a small handful of churches hereabouts. St Dyfrig, otherwise known as St Dubricius, was a sixth-century Welsh prince who established religious communities and colleges in several places between the Wye and the Black Mountains; he rose to become the first bishop of Llandaff, and died on the island of saints, Bardsey Island in north-west Wales.

A long lane leads to Hoarwithy, close beside the Wye, with a view ahead to the tall ferryman's house above the river – it became the toll house when an iron bridge replaced the ferry in the 1880s. At Hoarwithy there's a surprise: an Italianate church, complete with tall and slender campanile, sits high above the Wye on the hillside. William Poole, the vicar here from 1854 for more than half a century, spent his own family money on St Catherine's, turning a dilapidated chapel into a glowing slice of Italy. You climb steep steps towards a vista of telescoping arches under the campanile, a cloistered walkway into a church whose chief glories are clustered at the eastern end – marble columns, mosaic flooring, romanesque windows, an altar inlaid with shining blue lapis lazuli, a mosaic on a sparkling gold background of Christ in glory up in the curved roof of the apse. Prebendary Poole cast his net far and wide for craftsmen to work on his church; the master carver, Harry Hems of Exeter, left his modest signature on the end of a barrel in a scene from the life of St Dubricius carved on the prayer desk. If all this exotic

In total contrast to the Norman and medieval churches that abound in Herefordshire, J. P. Seddon's Italian romanesque church at Hoarwithy, complete with campanile, was built for Reverend William Poole in the 1880s.

elaboration sounds florid and out of place in this quiet Border countryside, somehow it isn't – perhaps because it represents one man's vision brought to unstinted completion.

Across the river, King's Caple is set among cider-apple orchards, Herefordshire's life source. The church, on a knoll with a superb view over rolling country, was built with a nave wide enough to accommodate King John and his companions on their hunting trips to the Royal Forest here. There are fine old box pews in the Aramstone Chapel on the north side, and some waspish handwritten church notes on the wall: 'There used to be a three decker Pulpit which was dismantled by former members' – here the colour of the ink changes, as if the writer at first thought better of his desire to name the vandals, and then took the plunge – 'of the Brandram Jones family'. In the churchyard wall by the gate a stone slab records: 'These walnut trees set by Rich + Prichard, Tho: Colley, Jo: Merrick 1681'. But the trees are long gone.

A narrow road winds from King's Caple out of a great 3-mile (5-km) loop of the Wye, by way of two more church-and-farmhouse settings. A side lane leads down to Much Fawley perched right beside the river, a solid red farmhouse with solid red barns and the little Norman chapel of St John's, which was saved from closure by a determined group of parishioners. At Sollers Hope church, further along the road, the congregation can hardly be much bigger, for it lies at the end of the track to the beautiful black-and-white Court Farm, the nearest villages 2 miles (3 km) away or more. The collection of medieval stone coffin lids in the church, carved with crosses and likenesses of mailed and helmeted knights, is striking enough, but more remarkable still are the 600-year-old timber frame of the roof and the stone walls still clearly marked with the fourteenth-century masons' chisel strokes, preserved almost in their original condition under coats of plaster until revealed during a Victorian restoration. Don't hurry away from this lovely spot; for church and court in their lonely fold of ground mark a parting with the Wye, which is not to be met again for some time. Now you take a great 30-mile (50-km) sweep, at first eastwards by the A449 to Ledbury, then north-west on the A438, A417 and A49 to Leominster, and south-west again via the A44 and A4112 to Weobley. These three handsome old market towns of Ledbury, Leominster ('Lemster') and Weobley ('Webley') were each for centuries the social and financial centres of far-flung rural areas of Herefordshire. Leominster still fulfils that role, as to a lesser extent does Ledbury, while charmingly black-and-white Weobley enjoys the attentions of camera-clicking visitors in summer and blessed obscurity at all other seasons.

You strike eastwards towards Ledbury through a country of hill and steep valley where the lanes tangle and bend round, up, down and between the hillsides, a rounded upland bordered by three rivers – the Wye on the west, the Frome on the north and the Leddon on the east. The people of this tumbled landscape find it hard to give directions to a stranger who doesn't know their private topography: 'So you'll go up, now, by Cockshoot and The Spinney, then take the barn road by the phone box. Are you set, now?' Here the ground is still active and in motion below the surface. In 1575 21 acres (80 ha) of land on Marcle hill went walkabout:

> *A hill, of which the stories told*
> *That it had moved in days of old,*
> *Glid for two days, church, manor, village,*
> *Pump, barton, tavern, crop and tillage . . .*

These lines, from the poem 'Wanderings', were written by John Masefield (1878–1967), the Ledbury boy who ran away to sea and ended up as Poet Laureate. Hereabouts is the Masefield country of long views over rich valleys so often depicted in his poems. There's an especially typical view from the top of Woolhope Cockshoot on the dipping lane to Ledbury, across Herefordshire towards the blue humped backs of the Malvern Hills. The tall spire of Ledbury's church stands high above the hop fields and oast towers of the farms as you approach the little town which the young Masefield couldn't wait to leave – though throughout his long life it influenced his writing and infiltrated his dreams:

> *Mine was a little town of ancient grace,*
> *A long street widened at a market place . . .*
> *Within the width, a market-building stood*
> *Propped upon weathered quarres of chestnut-wood . . .*
> *The little town was pleasant to the sight,*
> *Fair, with half-timbered houses, black and white,*
> *Shops, taverns, traffic, market, in the street,*
> *And cobbled paving, painful to the feet . . .*

Resembling gnarled elephants' feet, the 'weathered quarres of chestnut wood' which support Ledbury's seventeenth-century Market House are still much as John Masefield knew them in his late Victorian boyhood days.

Closely packed half-timbering with plaster infilling, here prettily dressed up with bay windows added on the ground floors in the Georgian age, is one of the principal motifs of Ledbury's ancient streets.

That description exactly catches the Ledbury of today, though the modern traffic in the long main street can hardly compare with the carts and horses that John Masefield knew. Under the Market Hall, sailing like an ark on its wooden pillars over the town centre, market trading still goes on.

The young poet had already quit his home town when the Barrett Browning Institute ('really terrible' sighs Nikolaus Pevsner) first reared its ugly clock-tower head in 1896, but he would recognize as virtually unchanged the great creaky black-timbered structure of the Feathers Hotel half-way up the High Street, the Tudor gables and timbers of Ledbury Park at the top of the street and the rich Stuart carving in the dark wood panelling and fireplace of the dining room at the Talbot Inn in New Street. He might also recognize the local talk and banter of the townsfolk in the crooked little shops. But the

Filthy alleys, close and dark,
Where few could read or write, but made their mark,
Where men and women lived and died in tetter,
So little human that the dogs were better

have all been cleared away from behind the smiling, ancient frontages in High Street and The Homend. You can still find the narrow arched entries which led between claustrophobic walls to those slum alleyways that haunted the imagination of young John Masefield. The one beside the Horseshoe Inn was the entrance to the grim maze of Smoke Alley; still labelled 'Nos. 41–67', it leads only to a wasteland of brambles and weeds where the slums of Ledbury once festered.

Today's Ledbury is wholly charming, nowhere more so than in cobbled Church Lane which leads past picturesquely sagging and bulging old walls to the tall detached tower and spire of St Michael and All Angels. This is more like a cathedral than a parish church, with a great Norman west front, a magnificent north chapel encrusted with the ball-flower ornamentation beloved of the local masons in the early 1300s, a pre-Reformation roof and a whole clutch of memorials. Those commemorated range from a thirteenth-century priest to Edward Cooper, Archdeacon of Hereford in Tudor times, 'Grave, learned & wise', and Captain Samuel Skynner (d.1725) 'who was no mean proficient in maritime affairs'. Elizabeth Barrett Browning's father, Edward Moulton Barrett (of Wimpole Street), lies under a damp and slowly crumbling grave slab in the north-east corner of the church. The most poignant memorials, though, are those in the chancel to the three Martin brothers, born within four years of each other between 1878 and 1882. George, the middle one, died in 1908, aged 28, of wounds sustained in a skirmish on the North-West Frontier of India. His younger brother Alick was blown to pieces ('lies in an unknown grave') in Flanders, aged 36, during the last spring of World War I – and the eldest, Hugh, who had been slowly dying of wounds he had received right at the start of the war in 1914, gave up the ghost at the age of 40, just before the end. Their proud father erected the memorials, inserted in each the medals of each son, and lived on.

There are other relics of older battles in Ledbury church – the basket-hilted sword of a Roundhead captain, for example, taken from the dying man after he had fallen in Ledbury's main street during a skirmish in 1645. Prince Rupert of the Rhine (1619–82) made himself a hero that day, still admired and talked about in the town, by the dashing way he charged with his Hereford comrades along The Homend and drove the incumbent Roundheads under Colonel Massey out of Ledbury with their tails between their legs. John Masefield had heard the old tale:

> Prince Rupert's horse had broken Massey's rank
> And sent him flying, in our Civil War;
> Men found the bullets still, in beam and door,
> Rude, leaden lumps . . .

Such lumps are still being picked out of beam and door in Ledbury today.

Leominster lies 20 miles (32 km) north-west of Ledbury, and the countryside between the two towns gives long views over gently rolling ridges, among which steep wooded knolls stand up sharply. There are apple trees in most of the cottage gardens, and apple orchards planted far and near – this is cider country, with Bulmer's of Hereford the chief growers. Like Ledbury, Leominster is full of fine buildings, but it lacks Ledbury's clearly defined eye-catching town centre. The way to enjoy the best of Leominster is to park in the Etnam Street car park by the creaky and ancient Chequers Inn, and take a stroll around the streets and green spaces bordered by Etnam Street (south), High Street (west), Broad Street (north) and The Grange (east). Corn Square in the middle of the central part has nice Georgian houses, while Drapers Lane and School Lane are narrow old lanes with small shops face to face over a strip of pavement. From High Street it's worth walking west into West Street, not for any particular architectural charms, but just to see Leominster in its day-to-day role as the place where the farmers, housewives and youngsters from all the villages round about come on the bus to buy fishing tackle and groceries, get their hair done and then sip a couple of pints in the bar of the Talbot Inn. Broad Street is appropriately wide, a harmonious collection of tall old shops and houses, and Church Street's restrained Georgian dignity takes you pleasantly down to the imposing red priory church of St Peter and St Paul. Surprisingly large for a market town, it was built in about 1150 for the priory established here a century before by Lady Godiva's husband Leofric, Earl of Mercia (d.1057). The church's original west front and great nave are really magnificent Norman work, and there are two more naves to the south, added in the succeeding centuries to accommodate the people of the ever-growing and prospering town. Don't pass by the reapers, doves, snakes and round-eyed lions on the outer faces of the west door capitals, nor the inner faces which show bug-eyed pagan fertility gods spewing grapes and grain, and be sure to see the wonderfully preserved fourteenth-century priests' seat or sedilia in the southernmost nave and the nearby wall-mounted, pre-Reformation silver chalice. Also in the church is a fearsome-looking ducking-stool, a chair mounted on the end of a see-saw contraption on wooden wheels which was last used in 1809 to stop the gab of one Jenny Piper.

There's a memorable end to your walk in the open green space of The Grange just by the car park: one of the best preserved and most beautifully carved Stuart houses in

The stark, ridged backbone of the ancient Malvern Hills (OPPOSITE), *which rise to over 1200 feet (350 metres) above the Severn Plain and divide it from the Vale of Evesham, forms a constant element in the eastwards view.*

the country. Built in 1633 in the centre of Leominster, Grange Court was dismantled in 1855 as an obstruction to the town's traffic and lay in pieces in a yard until rebuilt on its present site. Just before World War II an American buyer almost clinched a deal to take the whole wonderful structure across the Atlantic, but the town council stepped in to buy it in the nick of time. Now it does duty as their offices, its open ground-floor market space filled in and its carved beasts, satyrs, gryphons, puff-cheeked zephyrs and multitudes of fish as fresh-looking as when they were first fashioned. 'Where Justice rules', says the motto that runs round the building, 'there vertu flow . . . like collumnes do upprop the frabrik of abuilding, so noble gentri doo support the honor of a Kingdom.'

The 'frabrik' of Weobley, 8 miles (13 km) south-west of Leominster, draws thousands of visitors in the summer, for this is one of the classic black-and-white medieval villages of England. Don't be surprised if white squares edged with black begin to swim before your eyes after an hour or two in Weobley, as after an all-night game of chess under arc lights. At least two out of every three houses in the village are timber-framed, the contrast of their opposing hues kept dazzlingly clean and fresh by proud occupants and pointed up to even greater effect by the scattering of brick and colour-washed Georgian houses among them – most of which are just frontages tacked on to a black-and-white building behind. Among so many lovely old structures, gorgeously set along a falling main street, it's hard to pick out special favourites, but Tudor House is a gem, as are the Salutation, Unicorn and Red Lion Inns. Just round the corner at the top of the street is The Throne, once an inn where Charles I (1625–49) is said to have stayed, whose ancient timbers are so steeply canted that the house seems to be trying to bury itself in the earth. Bell Square at the bottom of the street offers further delights to the eye.

As for the church – approach it from the south or top end of the main street to enjoy the full effect of the spire rising above the black-and-white houses, its great height diminishing those nearest it, making even such a large building as the Red Lion seem like a toy house. Inside, the church is rich in ball-flower carving, in grotesque heads (including men suffering from toothache and from goitre, and a fiendishly grinning king apparently slitting his own throat) and other thirteenth- and fourteenth-century craftsmanship. There's a touching stained-glass window in the north wall of the chancel to Evelyn Theophila Peploe, who died in 1873 aged 8, showing an angel kneeling down, in a very human gesture, to be at the same level as the little girl he is welcoming into Heaven; and a far grander monument to the Roundhead soldier Colonel John Birch, the trader-turned-officer and captor of both Goodrich Castle and Hereford, who like many before and after him exchanged the radical politics of his Civil War youth (he was one of the co-signatories of the death warrant of Charles I) for a more establishment stance in middle age – he welcomed the restoration of Charles II in 1660. Birch represented Weobley in Parliament towards the end of his life, and – definitive stamp of an establishment man – became one of its church wardens. His likeness on his memorial harks back to his sterner youth, however, in full Roundhead armour with one hand defiantly on hip and the other laying down the law with a scroll.

Outside the village, down a side road to the south-west, stands Weobley's best house, The Leys, built in 1589, ribbed with enormous chimneys, with strikingly carved timbers and pargetted panels in the central gable – a tall and peaceful house set on its own. These timbers have been mercifully spared the blacking brush. Left in their untreated, naturally weathered tone of silvery-grey, they make a subtle and restful sight for eyes stabbed to surfeit by the black-and-white clarity of downtown Weobley.

Moving south again on the B4230 you renew acquaintance with the River Wye at Monnington-on-Wye, where the little church at the end of a grassy path is overlooked by the heavy stone mass of Monnington Court. There's a lovely walk on a bridleway through the river meadows to Byford, another of those church-and-court groupings so characteristic of the Wye Valley. These tiny villages are sunk deep in cider orchards. Tinted with pastel shades of blossom in spring and the richer colours of the apples in later summer, this stretch of country is a picture. When the river floods, though, it can do so with ferocity. Rises of more than 20 feet (6 m) in a night are not uncommon.

At Letton, 4 miles (6½ km) up the valley from Monnington, the church of St John the Baptist is hard to find. The unmarked lane to the church lies off the A438 on the left (OS ref. 335465), just before you reach a sign to Kinnersley on the right. The key is available from the farm office across the yard. On the east pillar of the northern transept arch you'll find brass plates recording past flood levels. The immersion of 10 February 1795 was a prodigy – over 2 feet (60 cm) of water came into the building.

Higher and drier ground lies to the north on the A4111 road to Kington. The trackbeds of horse-drawn tramways of the early nineteenth century can be followed on foot through the fields hereabouts. The Hay and Kington Tramways joined each other at Eardisley, 5 miles (8 km) before Kington, where the Tram Inn at the top of the long village street holds relics of those pioneer railway days. Two other survivals are here, far older than any tramway. You'll never see better or more vigorous twelfth-century carving than on the font in Eardisley church – a really unforgettable work of art created by another of those inspired craftsmen from what is known as the Herefordshire School of Sculpture. The carving is razor sharp after 800 years, showing two battling soldiers in flowing woollen garments, one sticking the other through the leg with a spear. Their round cheeks and staring eyes are formalized, but tremendous energy flows from their movements. A writhing mass of stone tendrils, ensnaring them, represents the world, the flesh and the devil – who may be personified, further round the bowl of the font, in the form of a large lion, lashing his tail round his body. The tendrils keep clear of his limbs, but in a scene representing the Harrowing of Hell they reach out for a tiny human figure being yanked forcefully out of their clutches by a running, purposeful Christ, also bursting with energy. The sinner's feet are flying behind him through the air, such is the force of that rescuing tug. A saint watches more stolidly from Christ's right-hand side. Everything else in the church pales beside this astonishing piece of work.

Even older than the font is the Great Oak of Eardisley, which stands behind the old chapel on Hurstway Common, 1 mile (1½ km) west of the Tram Inn. Local people insist this is the same tree mentioned in the Domesday Book, which would make it at least 900 years old. I can well believe it. The tree grips the earth with massive roots, its 10-yard (9-m) girth three times that of any other tree in sight. All its main limbs have dropped or been sawn off and its top – once measured at over 100 feet (30 m) – has been blasted away by lightning, but it looks rock solid. Alas, all is a sham. Walk round the back, and you'll find a crack in the side of the Great Oak through which you can step into the hollow heart of the tree. It is just a shell of bark and outer core, its heart burned out by some long-forgotten lightning strike, somehow still raising enough nourishment to sprout a crown of leaves each year – maybe on to its thousandth anniversary and beyond.

At Kington the border is less than 5 miles (8 km) to the west. Hillier country lies that way, too, and the feel of the small town is more Welsh than English, as are the accents in the smoky farmers' bars and the slow-paced market in its flaring red hall in the town centre. Nearby is the cranky small museum where you can pick up well-written leaflets of short walks around the town that will introduce you to the layout of the place – church, castle mound and narrow, steep old lanes to the west of the Victorian-flavoured business end. By far the best walk in Kington is the one that leaves it for Wales, climbing up the broad spine of Hergest Ridge (pronounced 'Hargist' with a hard g) on the line of Offa's Dyke – no need for an earthwork with this whale-back hill such a feature of the landscape. Most of the weather up here blows into your face straight off the hills of Radnorshire, whose lumpy outlines over the border ahead make a dramatic and telling contrast with the view behind over all of northern Herefordshire – a meeting of lush, fertile English lowlands and harsh Welsh uplands. After an exhilarating 3 miles (5 km) at this height you cross the border and walk down into Wales at Gladestry: but there are two houses well worth stepping aside for on the way – Hergest Croft and Hergest Court. Hergest Croft stands just off the track leading from Kington to Hergest Ridge, a little way out of town, and from spring until autumn opens its gardens to visitors, showing enormous rhododendrons, rare trees, azaleas, hydrangeas and old-fashioned English roses. Sir Arthur Conan Doyle (1858–1930) stayed here while researching his Sherlock Holmes story *The Hound of the Baskervilles*. The tale is loosely based on a legend woven around Black Thomas Vaughan of Hergest Court, a large farmhouse 500 years old in parts, which stands above the River Arrow to the south of Hergest Ridge. Black Vaughan (his tomb is in Knighton church) was beheaded after suffering defeat in command of a Yorkist force at the Battle of Banbury in 1469. His ghost returned to Hergest, only to be shut into a snuffbox and thrown into the pool at Hergest Court. A century later the snuffbox was found and the ghost of Black Vaughan accidentally released to haunt this part of the marches ever after in the shape of a gigantic, hellish black hound.

Gladestry marks the start of a rewarding, roundabout ramble along the hilly Welsh side of the border. The valleys are more deeply cut and the hills more rugged than those east of Offa's Dyke. Over these rough hills in the eighteenth and nineteenth centuries the Welsh mountain cattle and sheep were driven along the isolated drove roads in their hundreds of thousands every year to the markets of Knighton, Hay-on-Wye and Hereford, to be sold for fattening and onward transportation to the insatiable cities of burgeoning Industrial Revolution England. Places like Colva and Glascwm, tiny and sleepy today, through which you can easily pass without a glance, were bustling, lively centres of activity then, based on their drovers' inns and overnight pasturing fields. A winding minor road takes you south and west through the hills to join the B4567 at Aberedw; and here, turning back east again along the B4594, you enter Kilvert Country – holy ground to devotees across the world.

The Reverend Robert Francis Kilvert (1840–79) – always known as Francis – came as curate to the village of Clyro near Hay-on-Wye in January 1865. By the time he left the village seven years later in 1872, Clyro, its people and its surrounding countryside had imprinted themselves indelibly in the very centre of the young man's warm and receptive heart. But Kilvert had more than returned the compliment. In the pages of his diary – not published until 1938–40, sixty years after his death – he had caught the place and its people at that point in time, with unique clarity, humour and humanity. For

The contained wildness of the planting, inspired by the influential Victorian gardener William Robinson, combined with many exotic trees and shrubs brought back from China in the Edwardian era (ABOVE), and the clipped elegance of the hedges and topiary (RIGHT), have made Hergest Croft one of the most entrancing gardens in the Welsh border country. It is at its most beautiful in autumn just as the leaves begin to change colour.

anyone who has read Kilvert's diary, the countryside between Aberedw and Hay, which the curate of Clyro so often tramped and which he loved so passionately, is infused with extra glory. Something – exactly what was never revealed – happened to Francis Kilvert at Aberedw on 29 May 1865, 'the day never to be forgotten when I walked alone over the hills from Clyro to Builth and first saw the Rocks of Aberedw'. These rocks are outcrops of Silurian limestone, rising in terraces of slabs and pinnacles to about 600 feet (180 m) above the River Wye; impressive seen from across the river, but how one would love to know the nature of the revelation that drove Kilvert to write so painfully:

> Oh, Aberedw, Aberedw. Would God I might dwell and die by thee . . . Oh, Aberedw, Aberedw. I never pass thy enchanted gorge without seeming for a moment to be looking in at the gates of Paradise just left ajar. But there stands the angel with the flaming sword and I may not enter and only look in as I pass by the Gate.

Along the B4594 at Llanbedr, outside the porch of the plain little church of St Peter, is the grave of one of the most remarkable figures in Kilvert's diary – the Reverend John Price, vicar of Llanbedr from 1859 to 1895, to whom Kilvert gives the name of the Solitary. How eccentric Mr Price really was is open to question: his parish was one of the most impoverished and run-down in an area not short of them, and for years after his arrival, there being no vicar's accommodation at Llanbedr, he had been reduced to living in three disused bathing machines. Kilvert found him on 3 July 1872, up in a cleft of the hills (a *cwm*) above Llanbedr:

> a sunny green little cwm it was secluded deep among the steep green hills, and until you came close to it you would not be suspecting the existence of the place . . . What was my relief when I knocked upon the door to hear a strange deep voice from within saying 'Ho! Ho!' . . . A strange figure came out, dressed in a seedy faded greasy suit of black, a dress coat and a large untidy white cravat, or a cravat that had once been white, lashed round his neck with a loose knot and flying ends. Upon his feet he wore broken low shoes and in his hand he carried a tall hat. There was something in the whole appearance of the Solitary singularly dilapidated and forlorn and he had a distant absent look and a preoccupied air as if the soul were entirely unconscious of the rags in which the body was clothed.

As for the interior of the hut, Kilvert was staggered by the

> wild confusion of litter and rubbish almost choking and filling up all available space . . . broken bread and meat, crumbs, dirty knives and forks, glasses, plates, cups and saucers in squalid hugger-mugger confusion . . . the hearth foul with cold peat ashes, broken bricks and dust, under the great wide open chimney through which stole down a faint ghastly sickly light. The squalor, the dirt, the dust, the foulness and wretchedness of the place were indescribable, almost inconceivable.

And Kilvert was no easily shocked young greenhorn; he was well acquainted with the poorest hovels of the poorest parishioners of Clyro. Yet Mr Price was a devoted and extremely charitable priest to his people. Kilvert had the insight to see through the squalor to these qualities in the old man, referring to him as an 'anchorite' and

The mystery of the Aberedw Rocks, that outcrop up above the River Wye, is deepened by the question of what great personal experience Francis Kilvert had there in 1865, one which he dared not impart even in his diary.

remarking that 'if the Solitary had lived a thousand years ago he would have been revered as a hermit and perhaps canonized as a Saint'.

At Painscastle, a little further east, the earthworks of the big twelfth-century castle sprawl under trees above the side road to Clyro. Many bloody sieges of this castle took place, particularly during its early years when the hard and brutal Marcher Lord William de Braose ruled here. Kilvert recounts the story of one of these battles in his diary, between the 'Giant of Painscastle' (was this the hated de Braose enlarged into a monster by local mythology?) and a Welsh hero named Arthur, whose lady love had been captured by the Giant. Kilvert's account features a grand assault on the castle by Arthur and a force of '40 men each 7 feet high', the accidental shooting by Arthur of his lover who had disguised herself as a man in order to escape from the castle, and the furious hero's storming of the stronghold with a battleaxe and single-handed slaying of the

The solitary peace of the tiny church dedicated to Wales' patron saint at LlanDewi Fach conveys the remoteness that Kilvert expressed so often in this 'fairy land of blue valley depths and distances and tufted woods'.

Giant. The town of Painscastle grew up around a later castle built in 1231 against Prince Llewelyn the Great during his rebellion, but by Kilvert's time it had declined to a village again. In the early nineteenth century Painscastle had been an important stopping place for drovers on their way east to Hereford market. The Maeswllch Inn in the village was once an inn and forge combined, where the drovers could rest while their cattle, sheep and pigs were shod with iron for the onward journey.

One mile (1½ km) down the Clyro road from Painscastle, take the side lane to the right, which winds up hill and down dale to the isolated farm of Cwm at the bottom of a fold of hills far from any settlement. In a grove of dark trees on the hillside above the farm stands the tiny church of St David at Llanddewi Fach, facing down a valley heavenly in its utter peace and quiet. I came here at dusk on a raining November evening, squelching my way along a barely marked path across the fields towards the almost invisible church. Inside the little building there were no electric lights – only a double rank of candles in tall holders on the pew sides, and paraffin lamps on the windowsills and hanging from the roof. Neither inside nor outside the church was there a single mechanical sound to be heard, far or near – just the pat of rain on yew branches and the distant barking of a farm dog. The sense of peace and solitude was perfect.

And so down the road and into Francis Kilvert's Clyro. Here are Ashbrook House where the young curate lodged and in whose rooms he wrote his diary; the Baskerville Arms, known to Kilvert as the Swan Inn, from which the sounds of revelry, country dancing and street brawling would drift through his bedroom window as he sat writing; and the church of St Michael and All Angels where he preached, and where hangs the only known photograph of him – a serious-faced, dark-bearded young man. One of the passages in the diary most characteristic of Kilvert's writing at its lyrical best was occasioned by the local 'Easter Eve Idyll' custom of decking the graves with flowers:

Saturday, Easter Eve, 16 April 1870
More and more people kept coming into the churchyard as they finished their day's work. The sun went down in glory behind the dingle, but still the work of love went on through the twilight and into the dusk until the moon rose full and splendid. The figures continued to move about among the graves and to bend over the green mounds in the calm clear moonlight and warm air of the balmy evening.

At 8 o'clock there was a gathering of the Choir in the Church to practise the two anthems for tomorrow. The moonlight came streaming in broadly through the chancel windows. When the choir had gone and the lights were out and the church quiet again, as I walked down the Churchyard alone the decked graves had a strange effect in the moonlight and looked as if the people had laid down to sleep for the night out of doors, ready dressed to rise early on Easter morning. I lingered in the verandah before going to bed. The air was as soft and warm as a summer night, and the broad moonlight made the quiet village almost as light as day. Everyone seemed to have gone to rest, and there was not a sound except the clink and trickle of the brook.

Hay-on-Wye is a true border town. It stands a mile south-east of Clyro on the far bank of the Wye, with one foot in Wales and the other in England. At one time, in fact, the town was divided into Welsh Hay and English Hay, and old border enmities were always strong here. No longer, though; these days Hay basks in international prosperity and fame, thanks to the establishment in many buildings in the town of the largest second-hand bookshop in the world. Richard Booth, the 'King of Hay', has the headquarters of his business in Hay Castle, but the millions upon millions of volumes have spilt out and along the streets into converted warehouses, inns, a cinema and other unlikely places, as well as into a good number of plain, ordinary shops. There's a well-attended annual Book Fair in Hay, and literary events of one sort or another at most times of the year. To leave Hay without a second-hand book under your arm is a form of sacrilege. But Hay is not entirely about books. In its climbing, winding back lanes and tightly-knit tangle of streets the atmosphere survives of an old town whose market has been held since 1233 and whose shops and inns still form the social centre of a large area of rural Herefordshire and Powys. Hay defends the crossing of the Wye and draws all local roads into it as it has done since the Marcher Lord Roger, Earl of Hereford, built a castle and established a walled town here in about 1150 in an attempt to block the efforts of Henry II to subdue the barons of the Borders. The Norman gateway and tower of the present castle are the remains of the subsequent stronghold built either by the unpleasant William de Braose who left a dark shadow over Painscastle, or, so local legends say, by his good and courageous wife Maude. Hay suffered terribly in the thirteenth-century Border upheavals, burned, destroyed and besieged in turn by King John, Llewelyn the Great and the forces of Edward I, and even then it still had to endure a sacking, burning and laying waste in about 1400 by Owain Glyndŵr. Fire seems to be interwoven with Hay's history. The castle has burned on more than one occasion since the addition of a fortified house to its Norman remains in Stuart days, the latest fire as recently as 1977. Francis Kilvert was a frequent visitor at Hay Castle. He was friendly with the family of Mr Bevan, the vicar of Hay, who lived there, and often called in to enjoy a game of croquet and tea on the lawn – rather a satisfying social fillip for an obscure and impoverished curate.

From Hay a long and wild road south climbs slowly and steadily into long and wild country. It's a good 6 miles (10 km) to the top of the Gospel Pass at nearly 1800 feet (550 m), and the landscape becomes progressively lonelier, harder and more wind-blown. As the road winds over the lumpy hills south of Hay and leaves them behind, the imposing downward and outward curve of Hay Bluff pokes up ahead, paired by the rocky face of the Twmpa. These two noble bluffs are the ends of two great hill ridges, Hatteral Ridge and Ffwddog Ridge, which march north-west from Abergavenny for 12 miles (19 km), rising all the time, until at a height of over 2300 feet (700 m) they plunge away into the Wye Valley. If these ridges look formidable from down on the road, there are two more to the south-west even higher, more remote and harder to reach – the Gader Ridge and Allt-Mawr (the Great Cliff). All four ridges, and the deep, often sunless and in many places roadless valleys between them, are collectively known as the Black Mountains. Much of their rock is old red sandstone, up to 10,000 feet (3000 m) thick, but when the sun is in and the low clouds and rain are plastered across their heights you will appreciate the aptness of their name. Yet among their fastnesses are some of the most wildly beautiful places in the Welsh Borders. Ways of life persist among the remote farmsteads which have long vanished from most other parts of the Borders. Don't hurry through the meandering exploration suggested here. Take time to wander up side paths, drop into lonely pubs and chat over gates and garden walls. No time spent in this way is wasted time in the Black Mountains.

Hay-on-Wye, a mecca for the serious and browsing buyer of second-hand books (ABOVE), where the old market town's buildings seem to be mainly dedicated to the sale of old volumes. The other attractions of this centuries-old Border town are none the less enjoyable for being less conspicuous. (RIGHT).

Bwlch is a good word to know in this part of the world. It means a pass or place to get through, and the Gospel Pass is a superb *bwlch* – Bwlch-yr-Efengel 'the Pass of the Evangelist'. Between outcrops and cliffs of rock the road slips up and over the spot where, if legend can be believed, Saint Peter and Saint Paul once trod. The two saints had set out to take the gospel to Spain, but a storm had blown them off course to fetch up in this cold and foggy island. Nothing daunted, they girded their loins and marched out to do spiritual battle with the heathen Welsh. I'd like to think they took a moment to lower their gaze from Heaven and enjoy the wonderful view from up here, back over the Wye Valley to the hills of Wales and forward into the Vale of Ewyas between its soaring flanks of Hatteral and Ffwddog. Down through the head of the Vale of Ewyas runs today's narrow road, curling down through trees and between stone walls to reach the River Honddu in the valley bottom at Capel-y-ffin, the settlement galvanized a hundred years ago by the personal vision of a crazed and holy contemporary saint.

The Reverend Joseph Lyne had already made a name for himself in church circles as a hot-to-handle oddball when in 1869 he bought 34 acres (14 ha) here at the head of the lonely valley for the purpose of establishing a Benedictine monastic community. The bishops of Norwich and London had both crossed swords with him over his insistence on wearing a Benedictine monk's habit and his efforts to set up a contemplative order; but Father Ignatius, as he came to be called, was not to be frustrated in his single-minded desire. At Capel-y-ffin in 1870 he and his followers built a monastery – Kilvert walked over to have a look at the work, and wrote a long and fascinating account in his diary about his meeting with Father Ignatius – and by 1872 had started work on the church. Its sad and magnificent ruins still stand in the grounds of The Grange Farm up a side road below the chapel of Capel-y-ffin, roofless and crumbling, the arches of the choir tall and complete, its gravelled floor carrying the tiled grave slab of its founder. After his death in 1908 the community fell apart, as did the half-completed church. The sculptor and artist Eric Gill bought the monastery in 1924 and worked here for a few years – in the building is the little chapel he created, with his Latin lettering still clear on the beams. Nowadays the monastery is a private house, the great church a poignant ruin. In the driveway stands a large statue of the Virgin Mary, on the spot where on an August evening in 1880 four boys saw the figure of a veiled woman, surrounded by a dazzling halo, hold its hands up in blessing before slipping through a bush and disappearing.

The monastery was named Llanthony Tertia in homage to a far greater one whose ruins lie 3 miles (5 km) further down the valley. A good footpath connects the two, reached by a stony path above The Grange that climbs to the 1000-foot (300-m) mark and runs along the hillside with fine views down into the Vale of Ewyas and back towards the slope of the Twmpa. Llanthony Priory's ruins – arches and towers of the priory church – rise gracefully from a green sward on the far side of the River Honddu. If tourists do penetrate into the valley in summer, it's Llanthony that they come to see. You can drink and eat in the vaulted cellar of the Abbot's parlour, and sleep in a four-poster in a room in the north-west tower of the church, for the Abbey Hotel has been incorporated into the

The Black Mountains (OPPOSITE), *with their deeply incised, dark and remote valleys, are an ever-present feature of this landscape, their look, welcoming and forbidding by turns, reflecting the prevailing weather.*

The 'dim grey pile' of the ruins of Llanthony Abbey, 'by the river side among its brilliant green meadow', was how Francis Kilvert described it in 1870 – although even then tourists marred its solitude.

ruins for over 200 years. Kilvert came here, too, walking over from Clyro with his brother Perch on Midsummer Day 1870 and finding the tenants of the estate waiting impatiently for their Rent Day dinner, 'walking about lashing their tails, growling and snuffing up the scent of food hungrily like Welsh wolves'. The Kilvert brothers must have been hungry after their 12 miles (19 km) over the hills; they ate 18 eggs 'and a proportionate amount of bread, cheese, butter and beer'. In Kilvert's day the ruins and estate of Llanthony were still in the hands of the Landor family. The poet Walter Savage Landor (1775–1864) had bought the estate in 1807, intending to revive it, resuscitate the farming, plant trees all over the hillsides and build a splendid house. The trees were planted (many of them still beautify the Vale of Ewyas today), but Walter Savage Landor's other plans all fell by the wayside. He left Llanthony in 1813 after six years of waste and bitterness, having been roundly cheated and frustrated by the Welsh tenant farmers whom he had alienated with his autocratic ways and bad temper. During one vitriolic squabble with a tenant he was thrown bodily out of a first-floor window – a broad enough hint, one would have thought.

St David is said to have built a chapel here in the sixth century, living on wild leeks in prayer and solitude. In AD 1100 William de Lacy, a Norman knight on a hunting expedition, wandered into the Vale of Ewyas and stumbled upon the ruins of St David's chapel. He experienced a Pauline conversion on the spot, vowing to rebuild the chapel and live there as a hermit, never afterwards removing his armour which rusted solid and made a suitably self-admonitory undergarment for the hair shirt he wore on top. Soon William the Anchorite was joined by a handful of fellow hermits, and they established a simple religious community, forbearing to clear the trees or till the ground. The church they built has long vanished, and the monks of that early community themselves stayed only 30 years before the loneliness, the bad weather and the wild men of the Black Mountains drove them away to start again at Gloucester. But in 1175 some of them returned and set about building the monastery and church whose ruins stand today. Things went well for a time, and Llanthony held lands all over the district, but the lawlessness of the Borders and the constant skirmishing and rebellion gave the monks few periods of peace and contemplation. Owain Glyndŵr's uprising in 1400 threw everything into fresh turmoil. Rents could not be collected, and workmen were not to be enticed to the priory to work on its upkeep. The isolated community and its buildings began to fall apart, and by the time of the Reformation were already far gone in decay. When the priory and estate were sold to the Arnolde family in 1538, it was a merciful death-blow for Llanthony.

There is a wonderful ridge walk from the ruins, striking up the hill behind them to join Offa's Dyke on the crest of Hatteral Ridge. Here you turn north-west and walk up above the Vale of Ewyas for about 5 miles (8 km), Wales on your left and England on your right, with long views into the valleys, across to the wilder parallel ridges of Gader and Allt-Mawr, and forward along the ever-rising crest to its high point at Hay Bluff where at 2300 feet (700 m) the vista west into the Welsh hills is stunning.

Llanthony marks the start of an exploration of the north-eastern valleys that flank the Black Mountains, a winding and burrowing route up and down the vales, up and over their connecting ridges, the landscape flattening all the time – though never anything less than impressively rolling. This is lonely country where tourists are very few and far between; where elderly farmers in outpost farms still rise at five, lace their tea with whisky and hump bales up hillsides till dusk. Farmers are given their farm names as surnames – George the Vision, Bill the Cwm. Like miners on a day shift, the children of these valleys never catch sight of their home farms or villages in daylight during winter weekdays – they are off on the long school bus journey down to Hereford or Abergavenny well before day, and return long after nightfall. Pony-trekking enterprises help out the often stretched economies of the farms, and offer an excellent way of reaching high ground and hidden places. The Neuadd farm at Cwmyoy is well recommended, both for mounts and for expert guidance. All the places covered by this roundabout exploration, however, are accessible by car, though you'll have thoroughly tested the low register of your gear-box by the time you reach the Golden Valley. You'll also have enjoyed a memorable church-crawl, for the churches and chapels of these tiny communities are rich in contents, in history and in their setting.

Tight knots of houses and farm buildings nestle in the close folds of the Vale of Ewyas, above which runs the long line of the footpath following Offa's Dyke as it snakes through the border country.

The church of St Martin at Cwmyoy, 4 miles (6½ km) down the valley from Llanthony, bucks and twists as if in motion, its tower canted one way and its chancel the other, like a tanker in a heavy sea. The churchyard gravestones lean in all directions on ground broken and furrowed by subterranean struggles for supremacy between crags of brownstone and softer old red sandstone. Heavily buttressed on all quarters, the old building staggers on through the centuries. There is elaborate engraving on many of the memorial tablets, which carry idiosyncratic verses that repay a thorough search:

> *Here I lies with my dear Babe*
> *All cover'd with cold clay*
> *Waiting to hear the trumpet call*
> *Arise from sleep to judgement all.*
>
> *Thomas Price he takes his nap*
> *In our common mother lap*
> *Waiting to hear the bridegroom say*
> *Awake my dear and come away.*

Below the church the Old Vicarage offers bed and breakfast. The place is run with cheerful informality by Christopher Hamilton, who will put his own home-grown lamb, bacon, eggs and vegetables on the table and talk as long as you want about local affairs, footpaths, viewpoints and people. His dogs bark you in and wag you out. A most hospitable host and house.

The road runs east in a curve from Cwmyoy, a delightful lane just wide enough to take a car, snaking between hedgebanks overarched by hawthorn, hazel and holly, by Pont-Rhys-Powell and Tre-wyn, to turn north into the neighbouring Olchon Valley, wider and more pastoral than the Vale of Ewyas. Before entering the Olchon Valley, however, turn right just past Pont-Rhys-Powell and drive west by Stanton and Cwm Coedycerrig to cross the deep valley of Grwyne Fawr. The lane rises sharply to reach a tiny church unique in the Borders.

Partrishow church – the church of Merthyr Issui at Patricio, to give it its full title – is hard to find, perched up high above a lonely valley on a lonely hillside, its thick walls pierced with tiny windows. Perhaps it was the isolated position of the church that saved its superb fifteenth-century rood loft and screen from destruction at the Reformation. Vine, grapes, leaves, dragons – all are exquisitely carved in honey-coloured oak, a blaze of craftsmanship to stun you as you step inside. The dark stone font predates the Norman conquest; its Latin inscription 'Menhir made me in the time of Genillin' refers to Prince Cynddyllin of the old Welsh princedom of Powys. On the walls of the church are medieval paintings, including Death as a skeleton with hourglass, spade, scythe and a rather peevish expression. There are more or less faded coats of arms and texts, a lovely, simple barrel roof and a grille in the west wall that looks into an ancient, narrow little chapel on the site of the humble church built by St Issui some time in the Dark Ages. St Issui, a hermit murdered by a guest staying with him, worked various healing miracles after his death. You can go down into the dingle below the church to find his holy well, or linger in the churchyard, sitting on the stone bench along the south wall of the church, and enjoy the view over the valley to the Black Mountains.

The gaunt figure of Death painted on the wall of Partrishow church (ABOVE) contrasts with the exuberant carving of vines and flowers on the rood loft (RIGHT), all rare and precious survivals in this tiny isolated place.

At Clodock in the Olchon Valley the church contains slate tablets recording an old squabble between vicar and tenants that ended in the courts in 1805. How much were the old tithes of farm produce worth in cold cash? Twopence halfpenny for every milch cow in lieu of the milk itself, decided the court; twopence in lieu of eggs; twopence for every barren cow. At Longtown the ruined round keep of the castle is half-hidden behind a farmhouse at the top of the long village street. Built in about 1200, it's perhaps the oldest round keep still standing in the country. A gallows stood on the castle mound; only two centuries ago the last murderer was hung in a gibbet here.

Above Longtown you bear left along the narrow lane, with the sharply cut, rugged back of the Black Hill ahead like a green and brown tent pitched under the wall of Hay Bluff. St Peter's church at Llanveynoe, a tiny Welsh-style chapel with a little belfry, has three remarkable crosses – an ancient churchyard cross of early medieval date with a grooved shaft and truncated arms, and inside on the south wall two much earlier examples. One shows a Crucifixion, with the head of Christ drooping in death; the other a plain cross, its slab inscribed with the marks XRC, IHS and the Greek alpha and omega letters, as well as the engraver's own signature in runic writing: *Haefdur fecit crucem istam* ('Haefdur made that cross'). Tenth-century Hiberno-Saxon work, says the notice on the wall.

Keep bearing left, to drop down to the bottom of the Olchon Valley and up on to the far hillside with the Hatteral Ridge suddenly looming close on your left and looking like a formidable wall. Electricity did not reach this far up the valley until the late 1970s. The lane runs up past small farms, their sheep nibbling in the verges, to the head of the valley, where just short of the last farm of Upper Blaen it doubles back on itself over the Olchon Brook. Upper Blaen is abandoned now, after all those hundreds of years of farming activity: windows glassless, door barred, tin roof askew and farmyard silent and weed-strewn. This hard ground and isolation have proved too much even for the legendary toughness and resilience of Black Mountain farmers. A rough track climbs from Upper Blaen to the pass under the crest of the Black Hill. Twenty minutes of hard slogging up the track will reward you with an unforgettable view back down the Olchon Valley.

Back at Llanveynoe you hurdle the hill into the adjacent valley of the River Monnow. Up at Craswall in the neck of the valley is the Bull's Head, one of the loneliest pubs in the district and one of the least affected by the outside world. It serves a village of perhaps 200 people, and a very scattered one at that. The pub alone would not provide a living, so the owners supplement their income by farming. The main bar is one of those at the sight of which any progressive brewery representative would draw a sharp breath of distress. You go down steps into a dark, cosy little room where chairs and a settee are arranged in a companionable semicircle around the old wood-burning stove in the big, blackened fireplace. The decor can't have been altered for 30 years at least. Bar quoits and darts are the games, but conversation is better prized at the Bull's Head. Drinks are served through a hatchway in the wall where the landlady hovers to dispense good advice, local gossip or directions as demanded. There are few pubs like the Bull's Head still in existence, so don't pass it by.

Behind St Mary's church at Craswall is a grassy hollow where local men once gathered to watch cockfights – you can still see the projecting wooden beam ends in the north wall of the church to which the spectators would tether their horses. Craswall folk would also play fives against the windowless wall, in defiance of the well-known predilection of the Devil for turning such sacrilegious merrymakers into stone. The plain little church stands in a lonely spot, but far lonelier is the deep valley further north where the ruins of Craswall Priory lie. There are no soaring arches here as at Llanthony. The walls, so hidden among trees as to be invisible until you are right beside them, are not much more than head height, yet in the remoteness of their setting and their distance from all tourist hustle and bustle they are, to my mind, equally impressive. Here, half filled with drifts of earth, its stubs of walls bending under the weight of huge yew trees, is the starkly open shell of a smallish monastic church built in 1225, with a rounded apse at its eastern end, flanked by chapels and further to the south by cloister and chapter house. Craswall Priory housed a community of the Grandmont Order, a rare one in Britain, harsh in its observances. Roughly built of roughly hewn stones, the ruins of their church and monastery in this deep, damp valley have little in common with the richness of Llanthony and the other great monastic communities of the Borders. Tintern and all its glories might be in another world. Over these seldom visited, shattered remains is a profound peace, melancholy rather than soothing, as nature inexorably invades and obliterates the works of the Grandmont monks.

Two more churches lie along the road to the Golden Valley, each with a special treasure inside. Over in the valley of the Escley Brook, St Michael's church at Michaelchurch Escley has a rare wall-painting on its north wall, executed in about 1500. In black, white and yellow it depicts Christ of the Trades, a faded outline of Christ with enormous arms surrounded by working tools of every description – axe, spade, shears, plough, adze, L-square and dividers, wheel and flail, to name but a few. Such pictures were painted to remind working people that to labour at one's trade on the Sabbath was to re-open the Blessed Wounds.

Further east, up at nearly 800 feet (240 m) on the high ground between the valley of the Dulas Brook and the Golden Valley, St Margaret's is a beautiful little Norman church with a very Welsh flavour – a low-slung nave and chancel, and a weather-boarded square bell turret.

> *Turnips and carrots,*
> *Say the bells of St Margot's*

runs the local saying, referring perhaps to the cracked tones of the three bells before they were recast and rehung early this century. Inside the church is a truly gorgeous rood screen of about 1520, in silvery wood, exquisitely carved with intertwined foliage, fleur-de-lys and bosses with human faces, lion heads and flowers. How this wonderful work of art came to escape Henry VIII's edict of 1547 to destroy all such symbols of popery is a mystery. Somehow it survived, to glorify St Margaret's. In summer the church holds a flower festival, and then the entire interior is a blaze of colour. At that time of year the churchyard is in full bloom as well, thanks to the policy of mowing it by hand in the traditional way which allows meadow flowers long vanished from the fields to rear their varied heads around St Margaret's.

Now you are on the western brink of the Golden Valley, which runs north-west back towards Hay-on-Wye; but before exploring its string of little villages and fine churches, the jewel in the splendid crown of Herefordshire churches awaits you on the

The Tudor rood loft, covered with heraldic and naturalistic carvings, dominates the little church of St Margaret's, where in summer flowers fill the interior and the churchyard.

The late Norman stone carving in the tiny, remote church of Kilpeck, is the finest example of the work of a group of superb craftsmen who were once active in this part of Herefordshire. Their skill is to be seen in both the grand gestures of the intricately carved forms which surround the church's south doorway (ABOVE), and in the smallest interior details such as the expressionistic carving of human figures to be seen on the chancel arch (RIGHT).

far side of the A4465 Hereford road. There is nothing, anywhere, to compare with Kilpeck's church of St Mary and St David. Hardly altered since it was built in about 1136, the craftsmanship and wild, uninhibited artistry lavished on the church represent the absolute pinnacle of the Herefordshire School of Sculpture. When you consider how readily sandstone is eroded by wind and weather, you can only be thankful for the care that the masons took in choosing stone that has retained as much clarity and freshness as the astonishing carvings on the south doorway, the west window, the chancel arch and the corbels or tablets under the eaves. The whole church literally sprouts life and movement, with the south doorway the most lively of all. Smothered in a tangle of writhing tendrils, thick and thin, two soldiers stand one above the other on the west jamb in peaked helmets and belted coats of mail. Outside them a serpent wriggles, head down in defeat, while on the opposite side another one snakes upwards. Above these figures stands the tympanum over the door, where the branches of a tree of life bend to the ground under their weight of fruit, while overhead a double arch is filled with all the glories of creation: bulls, lions, snakes, birds, fish, beaked monsters, angels. Inside the church the artistry continues – three saints apiece on the pillars of the multiple chancel arch, standing one above another, dog-tooth Norman decoration over each arch of chancel and apse. Where the rib vaulting meets overhead in the apse roof are four wide-eyed, broad-cheeked heads with tendrils of hair and the pointed ears of beasts which, if they are meant to represent the four evangelists, owe more to pagan traditions than Christian ones.

Outside the church again, under the eaves of the roof, runs a band of corbels whose decorations make one wonder again just how arcane were the influences at work on the minds of the unknown masons who made them. Here, looking down in magnificent vigour, are grotesque and humorous carvings unequalled in these islands. They include a lugubrious ram; a baggy-eyed duck, a dog and a rabbit; an upside-down human face kissing a beaked demon; a viol-player; a pair of lovers, one smiling and one glum; a demon looking out of a leopard's mouth; a Sheelagh-na-Gig holding open her gaping vulva. If the Devil is frightened away from holy ground by church tower gargoyles, then here is a collection of grotesques bizarre enough to send all the hounds of Hell away with their tails between their legs.

Back in the Golden Valley, things are rather calmer. The village stands well spaced out along the River Dore, from which the valley takes its name – though in fact Dore doesn't derive from the French *d'or* ('golden'), but from the Welsh *dwr*, meaning simply 'water'. There are no impressive hillsides here; just a gentle swell from a broad valley to farmed and wooded slopes. The churches of the Golden Valley are its real glory. At Abbey Dore stand the tall choir and transepts of a Cistercian monastery church whose nave has long since vanished. Choir and transepts alone form a church too big and bulky for the little village it serves, built as they were in the century after 1180 for a large monastic community. Lord Scudamore carried out a thorough restoration of the remains of Dore Abbey in the 1630s after a century of decay following the dissolution of the monastery, and the transept murals, screen, ceiling, tower and east window glass showing the Ascension all date from then. But the enormous Norman interior, barn-like and soaring, dominates all this later work. Just across the River Dore is the old house of Abbey Dore Court, its walled garden open to the public and displaying a big collection of euphorbia and other herbaceous plants, clematis, fuchsias, primulas, viburnum and a

Although the 'Golden' Valley derives its name from the Welsh dwr *for water rather than the French* d'or *for gold. Its wooded beauty together with the glories of its parish churches justify its English name.*

host of shrubs and trees. There's a circular herb garden and a pond with a rock garden and a plantation of salix across the river. All this, and the restaurant, café and shop, are the fruits of more than twenty years' hard work by Charis Ward and her daughter Sarah. More botanical treats are planned for the piece of ground behind the Abbey which was once the monastery cloisters: the village people intend to reseed it with native wild flowers and manage it as a traditional meadow.

Further up the valley to the north-west, St Bartholomew's at Vowchurch has a superbly turned and carved wooden porch leading to an interior darkened by great timber posts like giants holding up the roof. If the posts originally carried the roof's weight, they no longer do so – one was recently found to be dangling from its beam rather than supporting it. Peterchurch, the next village, with its handful of shops and pubs, is the centre for the Golden Valley. The tall spire of the church, impressive despite its fibreglass construction (it replaced a medieval one in 1972), looms over the straggling village. Inside, the church is full of Norman work. Three great arches lead from chancel to apse, the result of a twelfth-century reconstruction on the ground plan of a great Saxon church built in AD 786 on the order of King Offa of Mercia – remnants in the shape of Saxon arches and stonework can be seen in the west wall and in the apse. Legend says that St Peter and St Paul, high up on the Gospel Pass above Capel-y-ffin, parted company when Peter decided to make for more hospitable country in the lower lands of the Golden Valley. Here at Peterchurch he consecrated a well near the site of the church, conferring baptismal status on its waters by dropping in a great carp with a gold chain round its neck which he had caught in the River Dore. For many centuries the custom persisted in Wales of keeping a fish in those holy wells used for baptism.

At Dorstone near the head of the Golden Valley a tangle of roads meets at the triangular green where markets were held in medieval times when the village was a Marcher borough. After refreshing yourself with the good food and beer in the excellent Pandy Inn here, leave the B4348 on a sharp bend (318421) and strike north-east up a steep lane which climbs and then falls into the Wye Valley. One mile ($1\frac{1}{2}$ km) into this lane, a left turn brings you to a pile of massive stone slabs beside the road, all that remains of Arthur's Stone, a late neolithic long barrow some 5000 years old. The capstone that covered the tomb, 20 feet (6 m) long and several tons in weight, is still supported by a few deeply embedded upright stones, though now broken into two pieces. This is a good place to stop and admire the view to the south-west – Hay Bluff falling away dramatically from the long back of Hatteral Ridge – before returning to the road to drop down to the River Wye at Bredwardine. Here in the churchyard between village and river, not far from his beloved Clyro, lies Francis Kilvert.

After leaving Clyro in 1872, Kilvert was never quite the diarist he had been during those golden years in his spiritual home. He helped out his father, the rector of Langley Burrell in Wiltshire, before taking on the remote and neglected Radnorshire parish of St Harman near Rhayader. In 1877 he came to Bredwardine as vicar, recapturing some of his zest for life and his knack of befriending his country parishioners while growing ever weaker in health. On 23 September 1879, aged 38, he died of peritonitis, contracted only five weeks after his marriage to Elizabeth Anne Rowland. His grave, on the north side of the church, is marked by a cross with the simple and apt tribute 'He being dead yet speaketh'. Poor Elizabeth, a widow while still a new bride, lived on until 1911 and even then was separated from her husband. His grave by that time had been closely flanked by those of two friends, and Mrs Kilvert was buried on the far side of the churchyard.

The church where Francis Kilvert preached in the last two years of his life is a remarkable building in its own right, with a sandstone slab lintel over the north doorway carved with two enigmatic figures – an elephant, perhaps, and a monkey – 'a puzzle to all antiquarians', say the church notes. The church is built askew, the walls bulging to the south so markedly that members of the congregation sitting near the tower wall on the north are denied any view of the altar. Many of the houses in Bredwardine that Kilvert knew are still standing – the Red Lion Inn, the fourteenth-century Old Court and the vicarage where he lived. These last two are best seen from Bredwardine Bridge, which is still threatened with flooding, as it was in Kilvert's day, when the Wye swells with winter rain and charges down its valley. The vicarage overlooks bridge and river in a lovely position high on the bank among trees with the hills as a backdrop.

The final run down the Wye Valley back to Hereford sets the seal on a tour astonishingly rich in noteworthy churches; it includes three more, each of which is worth a separate visit in its own right. First comes St Michael's at Moccas, set on a hillock in lovely Capability Brown parkland, looking across to the enormous brick Georgian façade of Moccas Court. The church is an almost unaltered Norman building,

Francis Kilvert was vicar of Bredwardine for a short while, and knew well both the rough-hewn little early Norman church (LEFT) *and the elegant bridge spanning the River Wye* (ABOVE) *about which the locals told stories of foolish travellers swept away in high floods.*

constructed of tufa, a kind of limestone formed of lime deposited by water around lumps of vegetable matter. The tufa has retained all its original sharpness of detail in the high chancel and apse arches, the windows and doorways, all built in about 1130. In the north window of the chancel is fourteenth-century glass in red, yellow, blue, green and white, showing tiny figures creeping around on the battlements of tall tabernacles.

Next in line is St Mary's at Tyberton, a complete contrast to Moccas. Here, apart from the Norman south doorway, all is early Georgian – an elegant red brick shell enclosing box pews, pulpit, angel lectern and an elaborately carved reredos in dark wood with torches of life, swords, rods and scourges, crucifix, ladder, pliers and hammer, axes, faggots; all this surmounted by a row of alarmed-looking cherubim and a phoenix arising in glory in the centre. This is one of the finest pieces of eighteenth-century religious carving in existence, designed in the 1720s for the Duke of Chandos, along with the rest of the church and the now-demolished Tyberton Court, by John Wood the Elder (1704–54), who built many of the best parts of Bath when the town was becoming a fashionable spa.

Six miles (10 km) short of Hereford the village of Madley straddles the road, another charming procession of half-timbered houses. The church is dedicated to the Nativity of the Blessed Virgin Mary, and in pre-Reformation days housed a statue of the Virgin which was an enormously popular object of pilgrimage. Chapels, a new chancel, extra naves and a crypt for the statue were all added to the original Norman church to accommodate the streams of pilgrims, resulting in a tall, stately and impressive interior whose treasures include an east window filled with stained glass that dates back at least as far as 1320 and perhaps half a century earlier. It features the trial of St John the Baptist before King Herod, the king's servants shown with wonderfully wicked smiles on their faces; flanking lights that include a lion with a squashed monkey face and a mane combed back and parted neatly down the middle; tracery and foliage from which peep out mitred bishops and hatless commoners; fragments of delicate hands and serene faces from a Jesse window pulled to pieces by nameless bygone zealots; and a Last Supper with a tiny St John resting his head on Christ's bosom.

A confession – I have consistently failed to find the gravestone in the churchyard to John Marsh, the pugnacious landlord of the Red Lion, who died on 12 October 1793. It's said to lie five paces south of the south-east corner of the Chilstone chapel. Perhaps you will have better luck, and be able to enjoy at first hand the inscription:

> *Famed little John a terror was to many a boxing blade,*
> *But now alas an insult brooks from sexton's dirty spade;*
> *For coward Death waiting the time till Jack was weak and low*
> *The moment seized and spite of art put in his favourite blow.*

Madley church is well cared for by its parishioners, who always seem to be about their business somewhere inside. You can enjoy a dramatic end to this Hereford tour by borrowing the key of the tower from the church warden and climbing up to enjoy the great sweeping view spread out all round. Hatteral Ridge and Hay Bluff are in the picture, of course, standing out along the southern horizon; and turning north you look over a great expanse of folded country towards the hills around Ludlow, the focus of our next tour through the Welsh Borders.

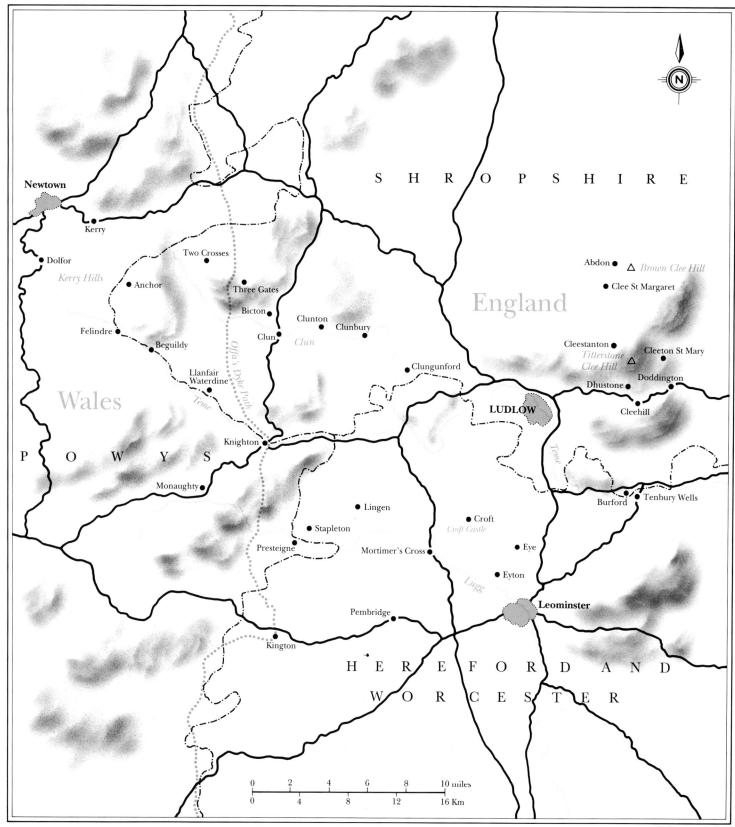

3

Ludlow and the Shropshire Hills

LUDLOW · HOUSMAN COUNTRY · CLUN · KERRY HILLS
NEWTOWN · THE TEME VALLEY · KNIGHTON · PRESTEIGNE
TENBURY WELLS · CLEE HILLS

The old Shropshire hilltop town of Ludlow may be a tangle of a place, but its geography is beautifully simple. The River Teme flows in a graceful bow south and east round the foot of the hill where the town stands; and the River Corve, coming down from the north to join the Teme, completes the watery half-circle. This bent bow of rivers is strung across where Corve Street leaves the Corve, rises to the crest of the town and, as Old Street, falls away in the same long line to drop to the banks of the Teme. Cradled in the river bow, the heart of Ludlow is still patterned by the squared-off grid of streets that grew up 800 years ago around the great castle on the western brow of the hill. Wide streets run up and over, north to south – Corve Street and Old Street, Broad Street and Mill Street; narrow ones criss-cross them from east to west – Church Lane, Market Street, Bell Lane, Silk Mill Lane.

Those street names alone give you a potted history of Ludlow: the broad thoroughfares brought the wool up the hill to make Ludlow a rich town in the Middle Ages, while the fulling mills and silk mills stood nearer the two rivers that carried the prosperity on the back of the cloth trade through the Tudor era. In 1475 Ludlow, strongly defended by its castle and town walls and thronged with influential traders and local politicians, was chosen as the seat of the Council of the Marches of Wales and for the next two centuries was the hub around which all the affairs of the central Borders revolved. All this prosperity left its stamp on the town in any number of remarkable buildings. Ludlow is a superb place to linger in, exploring the network of streets from Teme to Corve and back again with something exciting always in view. Dropping in to the Feathers or the Rose and Crown for a drink and a rest, you'll be surprised at the ache in your calves. The miles unroll unnoticed when you take a stroll around Ludlow.

Ludlow Castle walls stand guard at the western end of the spine of the town hill, a pointed sandstone arch piercing the blank face of the curtain wall. This outer wall seals in the earliest part of the castle, a tight huddle of Norman fortified buildings added to over the centuries, inside their own inner wall in one corner of the grassy outer ward. The De Lacy lords started the building shortly after William the Conqueror had given them the Ludlow lands, but it was the Mortimers who held the castle through five of the most turbulent generations in Border history. Ludlow Castle saw it all, often as a prison for unfortunates of blue blood who happened to be on the wrong side at the wrong time. Ludlow was a Yorkist stronghold during the Wars of the Roses, and here in the castle the two young sons of Edward IV (1461–70 and 1471–83), Prince Edward and his younger brother Prince Richard, were held for ten years until 1483. Then the two boys were whisked away to be done to death in the Tower of London before Prince Edward could be placed upon the throne to succeed his father.

Another inmate of the castle whose life was bound up with a change of course in English history was the 16-year-old Spanish princess who came to Ludlow as a bride in 1501. Catherine of Aragon had married Prince Arthur, the heir of Henry VII (1485–1509) – the prince was just 14 years old – and the newlyweds had half a year together in the castle before Arthur died of consumption the spring after their wedding. Soon the wedding bells rang again for Catherine and her dead boy-husband's younger brother Henry, a slim good-looker in those early years. But history held a divorce in store for Catherine that would be the match to the powder of the Reformation; while the athletic young Henry would coarsen and bloat, to carve his way through five more wives. Meanwhile the castle at Ludlow housed the Council of the Marches in a converted chapel in the inner ward, and continued in its pomp and power well into the seventeenth century. Milton's masque *Comus* was first performed in the Great Hall in 1634. The Middle Marches looked to Ludlow Castle for direction and judgement until the Civil War, when the town backed the king's cause and held out longer than any other Royalist town in Shropshire. Parliament made sure that Ludlow's influence was never as great again; and after the restoration of Charles II in 1660 its impetus was gone. In 1689, with King William and Queen Mary on the throne and a new era under way, the Council of the Marches was dissolved – the Lords Marcher had been brought low by Henry VIII some fifty years before – and the last vestiges of Welsh independence vanished. Ludlow Castle, its power and importance evaporated, was left to the dignity of dilapidation on its scarp over the Teme.

From the castle gateway a footpath makes a circuit of the walls, still impressively tall and solid, with views out between the trees over the rectangular green spaces of Linney, once the plots of ground held by the original burgesses of the town when it was founded shortly after the building of the castle. Nowadays Linney is a maze of bowling greens, tennis courts, gardens and tiny meadows, many still keeping to those 800-year-old boundaries.

Turning your back on the castle you look east along the wide open spaces of Castle Square and Castle Street. The Victorian Town Hall was demolished in 1986, making room for each Monday's motley collection of market stalls under striped awnings where traders hawk everything from horse brasses to monkey nuts. People come in to the market from far afield; elderly Shropshire farmers park their ancient Sunbeams, Rileys and round-nosed Austins along the pavements. There's a truly old-fashioned feel to Ludlow's market, magnified as you walk eastward out of the wide square into a squashed-up area where four lanes try to squeeze into one street's width. Market Street, High

The valley of the River Teme, upon which Ludlow stands, is a calm stretch of pastoral beauty, with grazing slopes rising up the hillsides from the valley floor to the wooded tops.

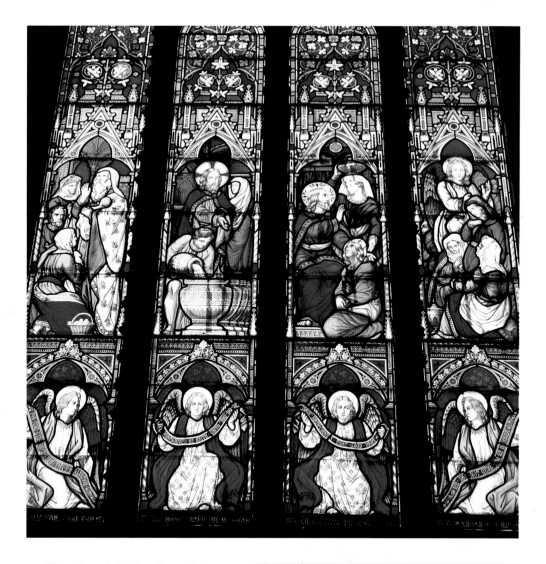

The colourful splendour of the medieval stained glass which fills many of the vast windows in the parish church of St Laurence (ABOVE), and the carved woodwork and half-timbering on the Reader's House (RIGHT) and on many other town buildings, all testify to the former wealth and administrative importance of Ludlow.

Street, Harp Lane and Church Street all run parallel out of the bottom of Castle Street, their separating buildings as thin as rulers. High Street is the rightful occupier of this space, the other three having solidified into separate lanes during the Middle Ages when the rows of market stalls pitched here sprouted cellars, walls and roofs to become fixtures in the old wide street. Whichever route you choose, you emerge at the eastern end of the crush to find the immense tower of St Laurence's church on your left, a beckoning finger not just in Ludlow but for miles around.

Rich cloth merchants of fourteenth- and fifteenth-century Ludlow gave practical thanks for their prosperity in the building of St Laurence's on the shell of the town's original Norman church. More like a cathedral than a parish church, St Laurence's soars to the heavens with great sandstone arches and pillars. Of all its treasures – including Marcher Lords and Councillors splendidly entombed, wonderfully sharp and funny misericords under the choir seats, and somewhere in the building the heart (probably in fact the intestines) of tragic Prince Arthur – the greatest one is the stained-glass windows. One north wall window has coats of arms from as early as 1320; the chancel of St John the Evangelist has a gorgeous gold Annunciation window of about 1450 featuring a high-winged Angel Gabriel presenting to the Virgin Mary, in a blue dress and red cloak, a scroll on which is written the Ave Maria, his greeting to her. In the east window of the main chancel (about the same date as the Annunciation window, and brilliant with purple, blue and poison green) St Laurence goes through all manner of unspeakable tortures during his martyrdom – being scourged, clubbed, whipped and roasted on a gridiron – before reappearing triumphant over death. There is a restored but still beautiful window in the Lady Chapel of the south aisle showing Christ's forebear Jesse lying on his side with a tree of life flowering out of his side to spread upwards, laden with kings and prophets, all looking up to the figure of Christ at the top. In the Welsh Borders, only the stained glass in St Mary the Virgin at Shrewsbury matches this collection, astonishingly complete, lively and fresh in colour – a treat you mustn't miss.

If you can contrive to leave St Laurence's on the stroke of the hour, the church clock's carillon of bells will play you out with a fusillade of hymn tunes.

> *Come you home of Monday*
> *When Ludlow market hums*
> *And Ludlow chimes are playing*
> *The conquering hero comes.*

said A. E. Housman in *A Shropshire Lad*, calling the wandering lads of his poems back to Ludlow yet again. Housman is Shropshire's own adored poet, thanks to that slim book of verses published in 1896 when he was 37. You can buy a pocket copy of *A Shropshire Lad* in the Ludlow bookshops, and trace many of the places he evoked so yearningly in his short, clipped poems of love lost, young life cut short and young people exiled from their home countryside.

Housman's own longing for Shropshire runs through all these poems; strange longing, since he was born in Worcestershire and admitted that his feelings for the next-door county were sentimental ones engendered by glimpses of the far-off Shropshire hills on the horizon. Yet one can't doubt the hold of this landscape over a man who could write these beautiful and painful lines:

Into my heart an air that kills
From yon far country blows:
What are those blue remembered hills,
What spires, what farms are those?

That is the land of lost content,
I see it shining plain,
The happy highways where I went
And cannot come again.

Housman's ashes lie in St Laurence's churchyard, and in the north-east outside corner of the church wall is a plaque engraved:

Goodnight, ensured release,
Imperishable peace:
Have these for yours.

Back in the tangle of Ludlow's town centre streets, the Butter Cross blocks the roadway where the four narrow lanes debouch into King Street. The Butter Cross, a heavy brick and stone market building on open legs, looks across at a fifteenth-century half-timbered house whose oversailing upper storeys lean well out over the road. King Street is wider than the lanes, but not by much, and things get tighter again as you jostle along the pavement through the well-named Narrows towards the Bull Ring, where Ludlow's medieval cattle markets were held. Old Street and Corve Street, wide and handsome, climb up the hill to converge on this triangle, once open for the markets but since then half-choked by yet another set of buildings – a row of shops on one side, and on the other the black-and-white court house known as The Tolsey where in the fifteenth century impromptu assemblies with names like the Court of Pie Powder or Dusty Feet would sit in instant judgement on any squabbles that had broken out at market.

It's a relief to break away from the constricted town centre and walk down along Corve Street. You may wonder at the elaborate way the Midland Bank has been dressed up in pseudo-medieval carving, until you look across the street to be smacked in the eye by the splendid ostentation of the genuine article, proudly displayed in the frontage of The Feathers Hotel. Here in a riot of carved wooden balconies, gables, beams, bressumers and posts, bursting with foliage and faces, Rees Jones demonstrated his importance to seventeenth-century Ludlow. Jones was – what else? – a lawyer, making such a good thing out of his work with the Council of the Marches that he just couldn't keep it to himself. And thank goodness for his showmanship – The Feathers is stunning.

On the opposite side of Corve Street, the Bull Inn is everything that The Feathers isn't – quiet, unassuming and plain in outward appearance. But go through its wide archway and you'll find yourself in a little patch of workaday medieval Ludlow – a squat and bulging range of black-and-white dwellings, an upper floor section sagging over the archway, a solid stone block of barns and stables very little changed with the centuries.

To enjoy a wider view of Ludlow, retrace your steps to the Butter Cross and turn down Broad Street. After the town lost its pre-eminence in this part of the Borders with the dissolution of the Council of the Marches, the judges, lawyers, doctors and country

At the hub of Ludlow's medieval grid of streets stands the classical stone-built Georgian town hall, the Butter Cross (ABOVE), which contrasts with the prodigious riot of shaped black-and-white carved timbering on the façade of the nearby early seventeenth-century Feathers Hotel (RIGHT).

gentlemen continued to build and live here. Broad Street is lined with their fine, dignified brick houses, all the way down to the line of the medieval town walls where Broad Gate's towers and archway still stand, the only one of the original seven to survive. The gate house is not very impressive in its modern disguise, smothered in stucco on the upper side and rendering on the lower, but it does loom satisfyingly large over the little Wheatsheaf Inn at its feet. Lower Broad Street drops on down the hill, a causeway raised above its flanking footways, to cross the River Teme over the fifteenth-century Ludford Bridge, far too narrow for the traffic it has to bear these days.

The south bank settlement of Ludford has none of the bustle of the senior town on the hill. Here the rush of the river is the loudest sound. There is a handsome half-timbered house down the lane to the left, dated 1614 on its porch post, with a wavy-backed roof and great fat chimney stacks. Below the house on the bank of the Teme stands one of the mills that made Ludlow rich; moss-grown, tumble-down and wobbly, the old mill looks down on the remnants of its weir, now overwhelmed and beaten nearly flat by the surge of the river.

Ludlow's mills are either ruinous or have completely vanished these days, but their memory lingers on in Silk Mill Lane, a narrow way running off to the west from Broad Gate, and in broad Mill Street which climbs again to return you to the top of the town. Along Mill Street are more of those elegant Stuart, Queen Ann and Georgian houses whose occupants kept Ludlow's economy ticking over after the Marcher Lords had left the scene. But before you leave Silk Mill Lane for Mill Street and the uphill climb back to Castle Square, spare a glance to your right up Raven Lane. This quiet side street, steep and narrow, could so easily be tooth-grittingly picturesque, but its practicality saves it from that. Raven Lane's houses date from just about every era of Ludlow's history. Some are so bent and bowed you wonder why they have not fallen down. The years have had their way with the street, and no-one has cleaned up or interfered with their effect. Twentieth-century garages burrow under sixteenth-century beams. Old ironworkers' premises, their faded name-boards nailed up, rub shoulders with small brick cottages. On the corner of Raven Lane and Bell Lane a wall carries a large advertisement in flaking paint for John Bowdler, Builder – an Edwardian artisan, perhaps a Victorian one. The narrow lane rises steeply, a jumble of houses and outmoded businesses that together form a natural and pleasing whole, a modest and unsignposted part of Ludlow history.

> *Clunton and Clunbury,*
> *Clungunford and Clun*
> *Are the quietest places*
> *Under the sun.*

These are probably the most quoted lines from *A Shropshire Lad*, though Housman adapted them from an older and – some say – ruder local line. He goes on:

> *In valleys of springs of rivers,*
> *By Ony and Teme and Clun,*
> *The country for easy livers,*
> *The quietest under the sun.*

West of Ludlow, the Clun country is certainly quiet – the silent hills begin to swell and grow as soon as you leave Ludlow along the A49 and A4113. The hill farmers might quarrel with the 'easy livers' part, though. As you turn off the A4113 and climb over the hills on narrow lanes, hard country lies ahead; the high-backed hills of Clun Forest, where upland sheep farming demands everything in the way of hard graft and long hours from the small farmers.

New and old buildings are widely spaced in the hamlet of Clungunford, attractively sited on its saddle of ground above the River Clun. Beyond the river the lane leads to Hopton Castle in a stream valley, a square stone Norman keep on a tiny mound in a field. Slowly crumbling, the castle faces a couple of farms and a close ring of wooded hills in this isolated spot. Sheep nibble under the walls where in 1644 a mass slaughter took place. The unwritten rules of the Civil War stated that defenders who fought on when in a hopeless position, thereby causing unnecessary casualties, could expect no mercy when captured. So when the attacking Royalists took the castle after a 3-week siege, having

A quiet corner at Bromfield, just outside Ludlow, where the huge half-timbered gatehouse is the only vestige of the buildings of the once-great priory that existed there before the Reformation.

had their offer of quarter refused, all but one of the 33 inmates were butchered on the spot. The castle mound was said to have run red with their blood. Royalist reports said that the victims had been shot; Roundhead stories insisted that they had been tied back to back, cut about to render them unable to swim, and thrown into the castle moat to drown. The Roundhead commander, Samuel More, was taken off to Hereford Castle, and later exchanged for a Royalist prisoner – a fortunate man.

Of the three remaining villages in Housman's poem, Clunbury is probably the quietest, a close huddle of houses around the church. Below the church an ancient wooden railway carriage sags rotting in a bush, its 'Smoking' notices still in place on the windows. Not much moves in Clunbury, except for the tractors filling the sharply bending lane. North of Clunbury you join the B4368 and pass through Clunton in a twinkling – a pub, a few houses, a muddy and ramshackle farmyard by a low half-timbered farmhouse, close to the river.

Clun, however, is a different kind of place – quiet enough, but the shopping and social centre for a sizeable area of hill country. Eight roads converge on the village, coming along the Clun Valley and out of the hills. St George's church on the north bank of the river serves an enormous, scattered parish. Here, as at Hopton Castle, Civil War loyalties were fiercely held and defended. Royalist troops so battered and burned St George's, where a Roundhead force was quartered, that a remorseful (and diplomatic)

The little village-cum-town of Clun, with its medieval saddleback bridge (LEFT) *over the river from which it takes its name, is the main centre for the valley and the surrounding hill country. The inexorable process of the drift from the land has left behind many barely inhabited tracts of countryside* (OPPOSITE) *in this part of the borders.*

King Charles II, when reinstated, ordered a special collection to pay for its rebuilding. It still looks like a fortress, though. The Roundheads had their revenge on Clun Castle on the south of the river: they blew it up after the war, and now only a jagged tooth of masonry remains of the big Norman building, standing 80 feet (24 m) tall on its mound above the market place. Between castle and church the village drops down on both sides to the medieval bridge over the River Clun.

Clun is another of those places best explored at leisure and on foot. A number of lanes run off from the main streets, each of which is worth following: Vicarage Lane beside the church, for example, which goes along the hillside between neat stone cottages to drop to a footbridge and swirling ford through the river in a little wooded dell. In the market place stands the Buffalo Inn where Sir Walter Scott (1771–1832) stayed in the 1820s while gaining inspiration from the castle ruins for his 'Garde Doloreuse' in *The Betrothed*. And along the street is the Sun Inn, its public bar poky, dimly lit, full of dark old settees and chairs, stone-flagged and devoid of piped music. You might feel like challenging the locals to a round of Tip It, a bar game I've never heard of outside this area. Essentially the idea is to guess which of six clenched fists on the table conceals a small coin. Be warned – with pints for penalties, Tip It quickly becomes hilariously disorganized, and you may find Clun not exactly 'the quietest place under the sun'.

A steep road leads north-west out of Clun, by Bicton, Three Gates and Two Crosses, into the wild highlands of the Kerry Hills. The views deepen and lengthen all the way, down into the sloping valley of the River Unk, up to high ridges where the wind does its best to push both trees and farms askew. At Hergan the lane crosses the course of Offa's Dyke, a brackeny bank running over the shoulders of the hills. The roof of these rolling hills is all moorland, a sodden plateau of heather and rough grass where snow lies early and melts late. At well over 1600 feet (500 m) you come to Two Crosses where five roads meet. Take the 'No Through Road' forward, bouncing and jolting on a stony track in among a great dark plantation of conifers, to find the hollow course of the Kerry Ridgeway running over the moor and through the trees. Unmarked and largely unwalked, the rutted trackway passes over these sombre hills in complete isolation; it's a rough old road these days, but back in prehistoric times it was the only through route between Wales and England high and open enough to offer some hopes of safety for the traders in stone and bronze who dared its lonely length.

Back on the B4368 west of Clun stands the Anchor Inn, a stopping place right on the border that was used by drovers throughout the eighteenth and nineteenth centuries as they brought their beasts out of the hills to the English markets. The Anchor itself – named by a sailor who turned landlord here, as far from the sea as he could get – is a small building, but just below is a wide yard surrounded by the sheds and barns of its droving past. Just beyond the inn you cross into Wales and pass under high hillsides to reach the A489 at Kerry village. There are new houses all round the old centre of the village from which in Victorian times a network of narrow-gauge tramways spread out to farms and forestry centres all through the Kerry Hills. Kerry's branch railway, the railhead for these little lines, was never anything like a success. The isolated village couldn't support its railway, which closed in 1956 after nearly a hundred years of obscurity. Kerry's church is another fortress of a building. Its tower in particular, built in the wild and unpredictable days of Owain Glyndŵr's rebellion, looks solid and blank-faced enough to stop a tank, let alone an arrow.

A marvellous story attaches to the dedication of the church in 1176. Bishop Adam of St Asaph and Archdeacon Giraldus Cambrensis of Brecon both claimed the new church for their own diocese, and on the morning of the dedication ceremony confronted each other in Kerry. Giraldus managed to get to the church before the bishop, and rang the bells to let the world know who was in charge. When Bishop Adam arrived, the two men each issued a threat of excommunication against the other. Then they both began to carry out the ritual at the same time, the bishop advancing towards the church while Giraldus issued forth from its doors with a procession of priests, a large cross and a vanguard of lighted candles. To make an excommunication valid, however, the proclamation had to be accompanied by the tolling of church bells. Giraldus had those

The drawing power of the capital, and the links through the cattle droving trade with west Wales, are expressed in this milestone at Mortimer's Cross.

already under his control, and when his supporters set to and drowned out both men's chanting with the prescribed pattern of notes, Bishop Adam gave up the game. Backing the winner in opportunistic style, the Kerry villagers who had crowded around to see the face-off hurled mud, sticks and stones at the bishop and his party as they rode away hurriedly with their tails between their legs.

East along the A489, Newtown lies spread out in the valley floor of the River Severn. Newtown doesn't make its way into many guide books. It's an old town, founded towards the end of the thirteenth century, and has a good sprinkling of pleasant old houses; but its great nineteenth-century expansion as a centre for the flannel industry has marked it down firmly in most people's minds as an industrial town, with all that that implies about lack of charm and cosiness. It's a pity, because Newtown is a fascinating place to explore, a town full of vigour and conversation. Coming down the hill outside the town at evening you catch sight of lights twinkling all over the valley. At the bottom of the hill the lights rise in one solid block, shining from ranks of windows in the Pryce-Jones Royal Welsh Warehouse. Now the biggest department store in mid-Wales, the warehouse began life in 1861 as the world's first mail-order company, the brainchild of local landowner Sir Pryce Pryce-Jones (you couldn't ask for a Welsher name than that). Big, red and imposing, with the original cast-iron pillars holding up the ceilings and a grand central staircase, the building sets the tone for Newtown. 'Patronized by her most gracious Majesty the Queen' proclaims the coloured glass window half-way up the stairs. The town was full of optimism when the warehouse was built, with flannel and other textiles going out by canal, railway and improved roads all over the country. In the 1830s there were already 1200 hand-looms in Newtown. The new mills, powered first by water and then by steam, brought a lot of trouble with them when they began to appear in the town – with workers refusing to use the new technology, and Chartist riots aggravated by bad feeling between masters and men. But in the 1850s a whole batch of mills went up by the river, and trade seemed assured. Newtown was badly placed, though, in comparison to the rival textile towns of Lancashire – too far from the coalfields, and too far from the sea ports which were bringing cheap, fine wool in from Australia. The Royal Welsh Warehouse was the swan-song of industrial Newtown. The local weavers moved away in their thousands to find better wages up north, and by the turn of this century Newtown flannel and textiles were virtually dead business.

To get the atmosphere of the town, leave your car in the big car park below the grand office building of Powys County Council, and walk to your right along the bank of the Severn, past old weirs rushing with water. Soon you reach the river bridge, on the far side of which was Newtown's chief industrial quarter where the mills and their workers' cottages stood along the northern bank of the Severn. The cavernous mills – those that have not been pulled down – now contain light industrial businesses, but the small workers' houses still stand along a maze of side streets and short, sloping terraces. Beside the bridge on the Newtown side is the Regent Centre, a cinema and nightclub housed in a square, plain building that looks as if it was built in the 1930s for just that purpose. In fact it was put up a century before as the Newtown Flannel Exchange, where for 20 or 30 years all the buyers in Wales came to do their deals before strolling across the street to dine at the Elephant and Castle Hotel.

From the bridge, walk up Broad Street to the centre of the town between the late Georgian and Victorian buildings of Newtown's industrial prosperity. There's a lively street market all along Broad Street on Tuesdays and Saturdays, where Welsh and English chatter and laughter mingle on the pavement and round the stalls. The lovely old half-timbered Bear Hotel, alas, was pulled down a few years ago in a move regretted by the townspeople. They gained a covered shopping arcade, however, well designed and spacious, where the interior of W. H. Smith's bookshop is a faithful replica of the style in which it was fitted out back in the 1920s, with bookcases of white-stained wood, a wooden floor, roof mouldings and hanging bowl lights of gas-like dimness.

There's a lushly over-ornate Barclays Bank in the town centre, from which the road bends up and down with a mixture of old and new shops, some shabby, others bright as pins, all bustling with trade. No-one could accuse Newtown of being tinsel-wrapped for tourism – with its many light industries on the outskirts, and new housing estates drawn up in a grand semicircle on the southern edge of town like Red Indians on a canyon rim, it's fully involved in the present. You only have to sit in the bar of the Elephant and Castle in the company of a roaring party of locals out for a night's fun to appreciate that.

On the little green opposite Newtown's post office stands a statue to the town's best-known son, the social reformer and industrialist Robert Owen. His long-nosed, sensitive face looks out from the wide collar of a greatcoat in whose folds a barefoot child shelters. Many such children had cause to be grateful to Robert Owen in the early years of the Industrial Revolution when they were no more than fodder for the factories' insatiable hunger for labour. Owen was born in Newtown in 1771, but it was as a mill manager in the crowded, stinking towns of Lancashire that he encountered the poverty and misery of industrial workers. All his life he put his money and energy where his heart was, trying to better the lives of working men, women and children through education, good housing, co-operative enterprises, fair wages and self-respect. He lectured mass audiences up and down the country, lobbied Parliament and argued his cause with sceptical industrialists who believed that drunkenness, ignorance and immorality were inbred in the working classes. At New Lanark on the Clyde he came closest to establishing the Utopian kind of working township he dreamed of. He almost bankrupted himself trying to set the same schemes going in America. He came back to Newtown, and died in 1858 aged 87, still planning his next lecture.

Owen's life story is well laid out in the Robert Owen Memorial Museum opposite his birthplace in the town centre, and down on the bank of the Severn his tomb lies inside beautifully wrought floral railings against the wall of the ruined St Mary's church. The church was abandoned in 1856 – too small for Newtown's growing population, it was already dilapidated and frequently flooded. The tower and walls stand behind the Elephant and Castle, enclosing a grassy space lined with old gravestones. Many of the inscriptions include the trade or profession along with the name – schoolmaster, bricklayer, gatekeeper, 'late of the Kings-Head in this town'. Robert Owen, champion of the dignity and value of labour, would have approved of that.

South from Newtown winds the A483 on its snaking journey to Llandrindod Wells. Following it for 5 miles (8 km), you turn off at Dolfor to run with the B4355 round the flanks of the Kerry Hills across high moorland where brown treeless hills billow away into the distance, dwarfing the lonely farms that shelter under them. Prehistoric burial mounds, ditches and settlement sites are dotted all over those hills, along whose slopes the Kerry Ridgeway runs as straight as a die. The B4355 passes high above the rocky gorge where the infant River Teme tumbles down to flow with the border for 20 miles (30 km) or more. Once road and river have made contact, they keep close together all the way from the bleak Kerry heights to the green and sheltered valley, where villages are few and far between. Buzzards wheel over tiny Felindre and Beguildy, each with its road-side pub and scatter of farms on valley sides. Below Beguildy you can cross the Teme, now a river rather than a moorland stream, to take the switchback, bending lane on the north side past farmyards and square fields with neatly laid hedges of intertwined thorn branches on top of their earthen boundary banks. The Red Lion at Llanfair Waterdine is a friendly place to stop for excellent food and beer. If sufficiently fortified, you may feel like a good walk – in which case, take the next lane to the left and park the car where it forks after about $\frac{1}{2}$ mile (1 km). Trudge up the lane to the right and on up the track at the end to find Offa's Dyke at the top (O.S. ref 257783). The stretch of the Dyke running north from here round Llanfair Hill is reckoned to be just about the best on the whole

route, with the Dyke itself standing 10–15 feet (3–4½ m) high, a great seam knit across the landscape, and wonderful high-level hill and valley views all round the compass.

Back at Llanfair Waterdine, breathless but exhilarated, turn down to recross the Teme and join the B4355 for the 4 miles (6½ km) into Knighton. Beside the road as it enters the town is the old school which has been converted into the Offa's Dyke Heritage Centre. Knighton – 'Tref-y-clawdd', the town on the Dyke – lies at the half-way point in the 168-mile (270-km) Offa's Dyke path, and Offa reigns supreme here. At any time of year the sloping pavements of Knighton clank with walking boots, and the shop doorways rasp against bulging backpacks on the shoulders of long-distance hikers. School parties from all over Britain make Knighton their base for explorations along the Dyke, staying in the Youth Hostel that shares the old school with the Offa's Dyke Association. There's a thoughtfully mounted exhibition in the Heritage Centre, to which the visiting schoolchildren add poems and drawings dripping with the agonies and delights of their outings in the hills.

As in many Border market towns, the centre of Knighton is marked – or marred – by a great rearing Victorian clock tower. Perhaps the architect could have chosen a more obtrusive design, but it's hard to see how. Nevertheless, as a focus for the town the tower does its job. The streets run away from it as if in horror, Broad Street steeply downhill and High Street even more steeply up. High Street pinches in its waist as it climbs the hill, seeming to squeeze shut with a snap as it enters a thread of roadway known as The Narrows. There are one or two antique shops in Knighton, but in the main the shops are still those of a traditional market town – family butchers, clothes and hardware stores, greengrocers and small tea shops. On Thursday the pubs stay open all day for the market, and this is the time to catch the proper flavour of Knighton as hill farmers in rubber boots park their Land Rovers half-way across the street and fill the pubs with their richly accented talk, a mixture of rural Shropshire, Herefordshire and Powys.

The Narrows climbs to join Market Street, which bends round the top of the hill, throwing off narrow lanes that twist down and away between the houses and stone walls. Wandering down these byways, you find yourself looking into side valleys running into the flanks of the hills, quiet green clefts where neither hikers nor car-borne tourists are seen. Knighton has many hidden corners like these for any visitor prepared to leave the car and rummage around on foot.

Our route now runs on south and east to enter the valley of the River Lugg. It may seem perverse, therefore, to leave Knighton in a south-westerly direction on the A488, but by doing so you can be certain not to miss one of the best moments of Border exploration. About 6 miles (10 km) down the road, at its junction with the B4356, you look down to your right on a great and – just at present – a tragic sight. There below the bank of the road stands an immense stone-built house, vast walls rising almost 50 feet (15 m) under tens of thousands of mossy stone tiles, a castle of a place. Grey, block-like and commanding, the house looks down the wide and lovely valley of the Lugg. Behind it run ranges of barns and outbuildings that form a complete township, a medieval

The River Teme near Brampton Bryan, now peaceful but once the scene of the bloody sieges of the castle. Brampton Bryan was stoutly defended by the pious Lady Brilliana Harley against the Royalist forces.

stronghold that seems to have weathered the centuries unmoved. Only as your gaze lingers do you notice the blank, unglazed windows, the holes in the mighty walls and the rubble of stones and tiles at their feet. The great house of Monaughty is a ruin, an empty hunting ground for owls and farm cats.

Monaughty was probably originally a wooden structure, the farmhouse of a monastery's grange farm, rebuilt in stone in the 1630s. It was home to a tenant farmer until the 1960s, but the structure was too extensive to keep in repair. The farmer moved out, and the cats and mice moved in; now the building (strictly private property) is unstable and extremely dangerous to enter. But there is hope for the great house in the valley, even in its magnificent and saddening ruin. The present owners have been pouring in money and time, stabilizing the building and preventing a complete collapse. It will take many more years and much more money to realize their ambition, to restore Monaughty throughout and open it up as a museum, but the results will surely be worth it: the house still contains its original panelling, enormous fireplaces and timber-framed lath-and-plaster walls, its kitchen ovens and Stuart dining hall, an Elizabethan wall-painting, and a timbered dovecote beneath the gables. May I be there to see.

The River Lugg runs east with the B4356 through its broad valley to come to Presteigne, a small town stretched out along the road. In its wide streets, big old hotels and linear plan are the signs that Presteigne once saw far more traffic than it does now. Up to the middle of the nineteenth century it was a busy coaching centre, catering for passengers on the long-distance stage coaches all the year round. The main coach route from London to West Wales ran through Presteigne, and the town rang with the sound of hooves, wheels and money. But Kington, 6 miles (10 km) south of Presteigne, took the coaching trade for itself when a new, well-made road was built there. Presteigne settled back with its inns and shops into the market-town role it still fulfils. 'I don't think Presteigne has changed at all in the last 50 years', said an old man who stopped to pass the time of day. 'It's extraordinary. Very nice for those who live here, though.' Very nice for those who visit, too. You won't be stuck for a choice of hotels in the town – the comfortable and creaky black-and-white Radnorshire Arms, with the date 1616 over its door, is just one of many that prospered in the town's coaching heyday. There's a relaxed air about Presteigne, its little wood-fronted shops and Georgian town houses, that winds you down and opens you up for a dawdling stroll and a chat with anyone with time on their hands – and most hands seem to have plenty of time on them here.

The heavy red brick Victorian Market Hall is where the roads meet in Presteigne. On the through route, High Street changes its name to Hereford Street here, while down to the north runs Broad Street to reach the seventeenth-century bridge over the River Lugg. Squat and solid, the narrow bridge puts out a couple of massive buttresses each side between its low arches. Flooding must be a problem in winter for the little settlement of old cottages grouped between the bridge and the splendid church of St Andrew. Inside the church is a forest of fourteenth-century pillars leading to a chancel whose unplastered stone walls give it a rugged but warm look under its panelled Tudor roof. Parts of St Andrew's are far older than these, however; there are remnants of Saxon arches and windows in the north wall, whose outside shows alternate layers of big stones and flat slabs laid by builders before the Normans came to Powys.

The church was the scene of that famous exorcism of Black Vaughan of Hergest Court. When his spirit had troubled the Borders over too many years, thirteen clergymen gathered in St Andrew's to put him to rest. They should have reckoned with the unlucky number. When Black Vaughan's spirit appeared to answer their summons, all but one of the clerics collapsed with terror. The thirteenth, however, kept his wits about him and managed to get Black Vaughan into a snuffbox after reducing him to the size of a fly – shades of Puss-in-Boots and the Ogre. But, as we saw on the Hereford tour, Black Vaughan was fly enough himself, content to wait a hundred years at the bottom of Hergest Pool for some fool to undo the valiant priest's good work.

There is one more nice touch about Presteigne. Though the days are long gone when any dark night might see the torches come over the border to set the town ablaze – as they did on more than one occasion – a curfew bell is still rung from the church at eight o'clock each night to put the little town to bed.

At the top of a secluded little valley to the east of Presteigne, reached by a long lane that goes through Stapleton and Lingen, two fragments of stone wall stand by a stream, smothered with ivy. These are the lonely remains of Limebrook Priory, founded in 1189, where six nuns and their assistants lived right up until the Reformation. In the steep bank across the stream are the scars of the quarry from which the priory stones were

The remains of Limebrook Priory, near Knighton, where a complement of six nuns once lived and worshipped. Even 450 years after being dissolved, there are still clues to the sisters' life to be found in this lonely spot.

taken; across the lane a damp, rushy patch in a field shows the site of the nuns' fish-pond. Their well can be found behind a wooden door among the trees on the far side of the field, clear water running out of the roots of a long-dead tree into a little basin.

The priory mill, now a farmhouse, stands just above the ruins where the valley narrows and steepens. The middle portion of this bent and aged house is the original mill, its bowed frame held up by an old stone cottage on one side and a tottering timber-framed building on the other, whose three storeys contain ancient wooden milling machinery reached by rickety stairways. When I visited Limebrook, I found the farmer trudging across the sloping farmyard with a sack of hay for the sheep over his shoulder, while his wife in headscarf and boots was carrying a basket of scraps to the hens – a scene straight out of a Brueghel painting. On a ledge of ground at the very top of the lane the nuns' Home Farm looks down the valley, a cruck-built house dating from the early years of the priory. The valley always escapes the worst of bad weather, said the farmer at the old mill – 'He do seem to draw it up and over.' The well never runs dry in the severest of droughts. Limebrook is the very picture of peace, its loudest sounds the rustle of the stream and crowing of the farmyard cock.

Under the hedge in the lane beside the priory ruins the nuns left another sign of their long tenancy here – the rare medicinal plant asarabacca, whose bell-shaped, purple-brown flowers grow from long-stalked, shiny leaves with scalloped edges. Asarabacca 'purges violently upwards and downwards', according to the medieval herbalists, and also eases childbirth.

Leaving this lovely spot, you run south and east along the lane to reach the A4110 at Mortimer's Cross, site of a particularly bloody battle during the Wars of the Roses on the Feast of Candlemas, 2 February 1461. A Yorkist force commanded by Edward, Duke of York, faced a Lancastrian army under Jasper, Earl of Pembroke, both armies agitated by the appearance of three suns in the sky. The omen turned out to be a good one for the House of York, who soundly thrashed their opponents. Four thousand were killed during the battle, which was followed by a massacre of the peasants in the Lancastrian army. The captured Lancastrian gentlemen were treated according to their rank – they were beheaded. One of these was Owen Tudor, whose grandson Henry was to win the final hand and the crown of England at Bosworth 24 years later.

Between the valleys of Lugg and Teme is a rolling, flattish country of prosperous lowland farms, bisected from north to south by the wide valley of the Main Ditch stream. A string of fine country houses lies from east to west across this gentle landscape – Croft Castle, Eye Manor, Berrington Hall and Burford House. Croft, Eye and Burford each have their churches close by, in whose monuments you can read the history, both glorious and tragic, of the great Border families who lived at the centre of affairs hereabouts: the Crofts and the Cawleys and the Cornewalls. If you are looking for a base from which to explore the area, you can't do better than make for The Marsh Country House Hotel at Eyton, hidden among the lanes and fields 5 miles (8 km) south-east of Mortimer's Cross (463620). Dating from the late fourteenth century, but with a much older house incorporated into its structure, The Marsh was abandoned as a ruin in 1980. When Jackie and Martin Gilleland found it in 1988, the house was little better off. But they have transformed it into a comfortable, relaxed and friendly hotel, centred round a hall as tall as the house itself. At The Marsh every little thing is just right, from Jackie's imaginative cooking to Martin's enthusiasm for local walks. With no previous

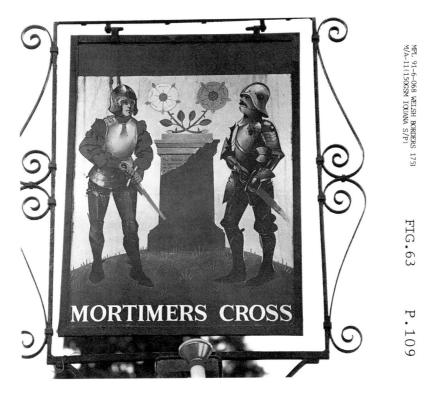

MPL 91-6-068 WELSH BORDERS 1751
M/A-11 (1500SM IOJANA S/P)

FIG.63   P.109

In the pub sign commemorating the Battle of Mortimer's Cross, even the ground on which the warriors stand seems to show the 'glorious sun of York'.

experience in the hotel trade – Jackie was a teacher, Martin a graphic designer – they have built up an atmosphere that combines top-notch efficiency and attention to detail with a warm informality. If there is a more pleasant place to stay in the Welsh Borders, I haven't come across it.

Another side track well worth making is south and west from Mortimer's Cross to Dunkerton's Cider Mill, not far south of the lovely black-and-white village of Pembridge. Here Susie and Ivor Dunkerton make superb Herefordshire cider out of a variety of cider apples – among them Tremletts Bitter, Brown Snout, Foxwhelp, Strawberry Norman and the king of the cider apples, Kingston Black, none of which has seen a drop of chemical spray and 70% of which are organically grown. The Dunkertons sell these cloudy and potent brews by the bottle, stone jar and keg, and allow a good tasting session to potential purchasers. They have also planted new orchards of pear trees for perry-making, and of the rare cider apples that are not wanted by today's commercial cider-making industry and which are in danger of becoming extinct. To watch the 'cheese' or apple pressings being squeezed of their juice in the big hydraulic press, or to stand in the old shed with a glass of the Dunkertons' sweet-sharp nectar in your hand as you sniff the heavily cider-scented air, is to take delight in a Herefordshire tradition not only continuing but flourishing.

From Mortimer's Cross, the B4362 takes you in 3 miles (5 km) to Croft Castle, where the Croft family have lived with only one hiatus since the Norman Conquest. Bernard de Croft ('Bernard of the Farmhouse') is mentioned in the Domesday Book (1086), and his line became great in Border affairs thanks to their friendships with English kings and astute marriages with Welsh nobility and gentry. Sir Richard Croft was one of the Yorkist gentlemen on the winning side at the Battle of Mortimer's Cross. His wife Eleanor ran the household at Ludlow Castle when the 'Princes in the Tower' were held there. Sir James Croft was Comptroller of the Household to Elizabeth I (1533–1603). Sir William Croft was killed in the King's service defending Stokesay Castle during a Roundhead siege in 1645. Hubert Croft, Bishop of Hereford, was saved by the pleading of a Roundhead officer from being shot dead in his cathedral by the Parliamentarian soldiers whom he was brave enough to harangue about their destructive and ungovernable behaviour. Crofts were always at the centre of things, while back at home they added, generation by generation, to the fourteenth-century castle that was their anchor in the Borders. Mounting debts forced them to sell Croft Castle to a rich ironmaster in 1746, but they bought it back in 1923, none the worse for wear and enlivened by a gothic front and a great hall built over the courtyard. Crofts continued to serve their monarchs (Sir Hubert fell at Gallipoli in 1915, and his son Sir James was killed serving with the Commandos in 1941), and though the castle was handed over to the National Trust in 1957, members of the family are still living there.

One of these, Mrs Uhlman – born a Croft – showed me round the church beside the castle when she found me wandering in the grounds one winter day. We inspected the tomb of Sir Richard Croft who fought at Mortimer's Cross – he also swung a sword at the battles of Tewkesbury and Stoke. Sir Richard's effigy is remarkably well preserved and life-like, with a commanding face set in severe folds. When the tomb was restored recently the skulls of Sir Richard and Lady Eleanor were found inside, their bone structure exactly corresponding to the stone faces above. Did another member of the family, Thomas Croft, discover America before Columbus crossed the Atlantic in 1492? Mrs Uhlman told me how Edward IV, an enterprising man, had sent Thomas off on a secret mission in the early 1480s to see if rumours of rich cod-fishing grounds in the western seas were true. Two boats made the dangerous crossing of the Atlantic and came back. Had their occupants set foot in Newfoundland while they were confirming the existence of the cod banks? No-one knows. They were likely to have seen land, at any rate. But the voyage had to be kept a secret – foreigners could not be allowed to learn of the fishing grounds that Edward hoped to exploit. If Thomas Croft brought back news of land across the great ocean, he and his king kept the historic discovery to themselves.

Down in the valley of the Main Ditch stands Eye Manor, a brick house built in the 1680s by one Ferdinando Gorges with the money he had made dealing in sugar and slaves in Barbados. Gorges was known as the 'King of the Black Market', and used his profits to enrich his manor house with superb plasterwork ceilings, unfortunately no longer on view to the public. The church next to the house contains a memorial more poignant by far than any of the grand Croft and Cornewall tombs. It was put up in memory of the three sons of Lord and Lady Cawley of nearby Berrington Hall, all killed in action during World War I. They were men in their middle thirties, in the prime of life. John Cawley, always called Stephen by the family, was a professional soldier, a brigade major in the 20th Hussars. He was the first of the three to die, right at the start of the war, on 1 September 1914. A year later his older brother, Harold, a Member of

Peace in the borders allowed Croft Castle to be turned from a strong and stern defensive building into a Georgian country house (ABOVE), with grand new 'Gothick' interiors and plasterwork ceilings, and large sash windows on each of the long façades. Only the corner towers give away Croft's former role. In the garden, too (LEFT), the National Trust's gardeners maintain the castle's sense of peace.

Parliament, was killed at Gallipoli. Their younger brother, Oswald, also an MP, survived the four years of war, to die in France three months before the end.

Berrington Hall stands down the road from the church, a great Georgian sandstone pile of a house with soaring pillars topped by an enormous pediment, looking over its gravelled carriage drive down a long green slope to the lake created by Lancelot 'Capability' Brown (1715–83). Now in the care of the National Trust, the house with its superb staircase and painted ceilings should by all rights be a pleasure to visit. But after seeing that memorial to the three Cawley boys who grew up here, one's mind is filled with other images – the brothers, 5 years between the lot of them, in their privileged, golden boyhood of the 1880s and 1890s, running over the grass, fishing in the lake, riding their ponies under the arch of the gateway; the telegrams arriving at the house with news of their deaths; Lord and Lady Cawley coping with the loss of one after another of their sons, the death of young Oswald the last crushing blow.

Beyond Berrington Hall the lane takes you on to the A4112, where you turn north to reach the once prosperous spa town of Tenbury Wells. At the bend of the hill entering Tenbury, the Pembroke House Inn leans back from its foundations, wonderfully canted and creaky, shabby and dark. Tenbury itself is a bit shabby these days, though there are some attractive old black-and-white houses in the town, and a handful of fine big

Two faces of Herefordshire building style: the spreading Georgian elegance of Berrington Hall (LEFT), *with its sad memories of the Cawley brothers who all died in the Great War, and the surprise of the dining room inside, decorated with paintings of Admiral Rodney's proud naval victories; and the gloriously drunken lean of the black and white timber-framed Pembroke House Inn* (OPPOSITE), *sitting back on its haunches at nearby Tenbury Wells.*

Victorian houses around the outskirts. Victorians came to Tenbury to socialize while drinking, and splashing about in, the saline spring waters discovered here in the 1830s. The spa was never a very grand affair, though; it was advertised as suitable for the 'middling and working classes'. A pump room and bath house were built in 1862, and for 50 years Tenbury did a modest trade in accommodation and bath services. But during World War I business declined, and never subsequently recovered. Tenbury still seems to miss that vanished trade. There are some handsome brick houses round the circular market house in the little triangular square, but many of the town's shops struggle to make ends meet these days. Wide Teme Street leads down to the bridge over the River Teme, its hotels run down sadly from the sleek prosperity of former days. Even the bridge, built on an eye-catching curve, sprouts weeds from the cracks in its walls.

Symbol of Tenbury's decline, the old bath houses and pumping tower are gently falling to pieces on their patch of ground behind the Crow Hotel where the Kyre Brook runs at the southern end of Teme Street. The tin-roofed, tin-walled bath houses, rusting and dilapidated, have elaborate ornamentation in wood and tin around their eaves, and entrance doors under pseudo-Norman brick arches. The pumping tower is crowned with a spire (which gave the whole complex its nickname, 'The Pepperpot') whose skeleton of timbers encloses the galvanized tanks that held the healing waters.

The best pub in Tenbury Wells is the smallest one, The Vaults in Teme Street. The beer is nothing to shout about, but this is where elderly men from the town and its surrounding countryside congregate to sit and stare at their gumboots. Talk in The Vaults revolves entirely around local matters, and here you can tease out local opinions about the town.

Just across the river from Tenbury Wells is Burford House, built early in the eighteenth century on the site of the castle where the Cornewall family held sway from 1304 until the line died out shortly before the house was built. Nowadays there is a garden centre in the grounds, a pottery and craft shop, all helping to keep the big, square-built house in decent repair. Beside Burford House stands St Mary's church, its chancel filled with monuments and memorials to the Cornewalls. Eleanor Croft, wife of Sir Richard who fought at Mortimer's Cross, was born a Cornewall, and like the Crofts her family was influential in Border affairs throughout the Middle Ages and far beyond. Under the beautiful Victorian angel roof of the chancel lie Princess Elizabeth, a Cornewall wife who was sister to Henry IV, and the young knight Edmund Cornewall who died in 1508 aged 20. The heart of another Edmund Cornewall is buried here – he was an adventurer, who 'travelling to know Foreign Countries, died at Cologne, the xivth year of Henry VI, and willed his servant to bury his body there and to enclose his Heart in lead and carry it to Burford to be buried'. Edmund's monument also commemorates his daughter, Dame Eleanor Cornewall, who had seventeen score descendants by the time of her death.

The most remarkable item in the chancel is the Tudor triptych in the north wall, painted in the year of the Spanish Armada (1588), its colours still vivid; a great cupboard of a thing, with the twelve apostles featured on the outer panels of the doors, the four evangelists all scribbling away at their books. Inside the doors is a tall painting of Richard Cornewall, who died in 1568, his wife Jenet and their fully-armoured son – yet another Edmund. Unlatching the long, narrow doors beneath, you find Edmund painted as a corpse at life-size length, all 7 foot 3 inches (2.2 m) of him, lying naked in a shroud

Tranquillity returned to Tenbury Wells after its few giddy years as a Victorian spa town. There is no longer the bustle of visitors coming to stay in the genteel houses of the town (LEFT); meanwhile, the spending power of modern visitors is able to maintain Burford House (BELOW), the plain brick early Georgian house built for William Bowles on the site of the Cornewalls' castle, which lies across the river – and across the county boundary back into Shropshire.

like a polythene bag neatly tied up at the top of his curly dark hair, his face with its nobly hooked nose pale and hollowed by death.

Travelling north from Burford and Tenbury Wells along the B4214 on the final stage of the Ludlow tour, you enter a wild and strange landscape, utterly different in appearance and atmosphere from the lush valley country of Teme and Lugg. Here in the south-eastern corner of Shropshire rise the Clee Hills, lumps of carboniferous sandstone rock with caps of hard, volcanic basalt, known hereabouts as 'dhu-stone' or black-stone. Dhu-stone has been quarried from the Clee Hills for many centuries, for building and for road-surfacing, and the quarrying still goes on near the summit of Titterstone Clee Hill. But there are other mineral treasures in these raw, rugged highlands – coal, iron ore and copper, as well as the limestone that underlies the black peaks. All have been mined and quarried since the Middle Ages, and the scars of these old and new operations emphasize the Clee Hills' already uneven outlines. The hills rise to 1750 feet (533 m) at the summit of Titterstone Clee Hill, and even higher on Brown Clee Hill to the north. Up here the wind whips through the villages – Cleehill, Dhustone, Clee St Margaret – that grew up around the mineral industries of the hills. These are not picture postcard places. Those who have never seen the mining settlements of the north of England find them grim, a nasty shock after the neat, half-timbered villages so cosily sited down in the adjacent valleys of Shropshire, Herefordshire and Worcestershire. Clee people have a reputation locally, too, rather like that of the inhabitants of the Forest of Dean – close, obstinate, insular folk who keep themselves to themselves. In fact, a Clee conversation once started is not soon finished, especially if it runs on the history and industry of the area. The further you explore into and over these apparently barren heights, the greater becomes their hold over you – particularly if you walk their multitude of paths and trackways. Don't turn your back on the Clee Hills, or you will miss an integral and highly-flavoured part of Border life and landscape.

Cleehill village straggles round the road junction where the B4214 ends its long rise to meet the A4117 Ludlow to Kidderminster road. Small brick houses, plain shops and a couple of workaday pubs – there's nothing grand about Cleehill except for its great southward view down over the Teme valley and up again. Turning left along the A4117 towards Ludlow and taking the first lane on the right after about 1 mile ($1\frac{1}{2}$ km), you climb between grass-grown heaps of coal-mining spoil through the handful of terraced houses that make up the mining and quarrying hamlet of Dhustone – a straightforward name, with the volcanic stone forming hard-edged ridges above the houses. At the back of Dhustone rears the crest of Titterstone Clee Hill, its battered brow quarried into great cliffs and ledges now abandoned and greened over. The heathery slopes of the hill are sprinkled with cottages, most now derelict, where miners set up house as squatters on small parcels of land, sinking small shafts and extracting enough coal and ore to make a bare living. Before the days of motor transport the miners' wives would carry baskets of coal on their backs down the hill to the road, along sunken trackways known as strakers. The top of Titterstone Clee Hill was all open common land, and the miners kept cows and sheep which they drove up the strakers to pasture on the commons. In the nineteenth century roads were built up to the mines, making life just a bit easier.

The couple of quarries still active in these hills lie immediately east of Dhustone, and by climbing the bank behind the terraced houses you can look down on their vast craters with orange-red rock walls where yellow tipper trucks and diggers crawl through

The font in the ancient little church of Stottesdon set in the Clee Hills is a superb example of the twelfth-century Herefordshire sculptors' work, still crisply carved with beasts and foliage set within ribbed interlacing.

the sludge below. From Dhustone the roughly tarmacked track climbs on across the shoulder of the hill, up among the quarry cliffs where ruined buildings stand on the ledges. Park here and scramble up the hillside through slides of quarry stone to reach the triangulation pillar at the top. A civil aviation radar station has been built up here on the peak of Titterstone Clee, and standing beside its skeleton towers and golf-ball shapes you can enjoy the view at 1750 feet (533 m) – south to the Teme valley, east into Worcestershire and the green acres of trees in the Wyre Forest; north to the bare Clee backs running up to Brown Clee Hill, west over Ludlow towards the uplands of Wales.

The enormous round bulk of Titterstone Clee Hill blocks the way north into the heart of the Clee Hills, but two side roads off the A4117 curve round its flanks – one east of Cleehill village at Doddington, through Cleeton St Mary; the other west by way of Bitterley and Cleestanton. Once north of Titterstone Clee you are in a lonely country of steep valleys and high hillsides, a farming landscape of scattered villages and farms with massive stone barns along little side lanes overlooked by most visitors to the area. Brown Clee Hill dominates the view here as Titterstone Clee Hill does to the south of the range. Brown Clee has been thoroughly quarried for its hard stone through the ages, but it lacks the rugged, domed and cratered look of its southerly neighbour. There is a smoother upward sweep to the flanks of Brown Clee, green slopes furrowed with bracken-choked coombs reminiscent of the heights of Exmoor. With great white clouds sailing behind its crest, Brown Clee entices anyone with a walker's heart.

At Clee St Margaret you drive through a ford that flows along the cobbled bed of the street for 150 feet (45 m) and turn left at the next crossroads to find Heath Chapel standing alone in a field beside the road. This is a quite remarkable building, small though it is – an early Norman church completely unrestored, devoid of tower or bell

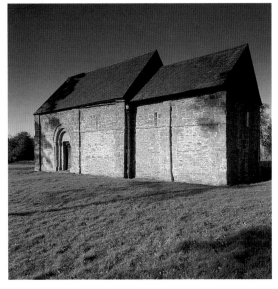

The mounds and hollows in the grassy fields at Abdon (ABOVE) are all that remain to show where the medieval and Tudor village once was, before the decline of local farming and quarrying caused its depopulation, while at nearby Heath the tiny, bare Norman church (LEFT) stands forlornly in a field, likewise bereft of the village which it once served.

turret, a simple structure of yellow and grey stone. There was never enough money in this remote district to improve or restore the chapel, so it has been left almost exactly as its twelfth-century builders erected it, with a round-arched single doorway decorated with chevron carving, a three-tier, round chancel arch and a cylindrical tub of a font. The flaking plaster of the walls covers a mass of medieval paintings awaiting restoration – St George on a white charger is over the door, fragments of texts on the north wall. The rest of these magnificent paintings lie hidden for lack of funds.

Heath was one of many settlements up in the Clee Hills to be abandoned during the Middle Ages. The Black Death played its part in this depopulation of the Clee uplands, but deteriorating weather conditions had more to do with it. These marginal lands never yielded more than a poor subsistence living for farmers relying on crop-growing, and one by one the farms amalgamated to create bigger units where animals could roam and graze. Those farmers too small and poor to take their place in the new system found themselves squeezed out of their holdings, and moved lower down the slopes to more productive land. The abandoned settlement of Heath can just be made out as a mass of hummocks in the field north of the chapel, but there is a much more impressive site further north, behind the church at Abdon. A gate on the north-west corner of the churchyard leads into the sloping field where the remains of the deserted village lie. A hollow, grassy trackway descends the hill, winding in among the platforms, humps, village thoroughfares and field banks. If you can make your visit early on a sunny morning or late in the evening, the shadows will help you make out the ground plan of the settlement. The village was repopulated for a short while in the sixteenth and seventeenth centuries, when coal-mining and quarrying on Brown Clee Hill reached a peak, but as the industries declined, Abdon was left once more to grow green and silent.

Ludlow lies only a short drive south-west of Abdon, but before completing the tour you can enjoy a final grandstand view over the country you have explored by climbing to the top of Brown Clee Hill. A rutted track leaves the lane under the hill, mounting steadily and steeply between high banks where wooden posts have been put up to show the route in the snows of winter. The top of Brown Clee Hill was never enclosed or brought under any kind of formal agriculture, and it still remains one of the largest stretches of common land in Shropshire. There are more satellite dishes, drums and towers up here, a useful aiming point as you walk among quarrying humps to the summit at 1772 feet (540 m). Quarrying on Brown Clee Hill came to an end in 1936, but by that time the massive ramparts of Abdon Burf camp, an Iron Age hill fort, had been almost completely destroyed.

There is an exciting end to the walk, with the eastern prospect hidden until the last moment. Then a great expanse of Border country bursts into view. Titterstone Clee Hill shoves its sharply angled snout along the southern horizon, while on the south and east lies the Wyre Forest and – if the weather permits – a glimpse of the dinosaur spine of the Malvern Hills. The view to the west and north is the best, though, filled from end to end by the long ridge of Wenlock Edge, patched with fields of different colours and dark green blocks of woodland. Over the back of Wenlock Edge rise other hills, marching away into Shropshire – the Caradoc Hills around Church Stretton, and beyond them the dimly seen roll of the Long Mynd. In the course of the next tour through the Borders you will be up there on those beckoning hills, looking back and remembering this heart-lifting moment on the summit of Brown Clee Hill.

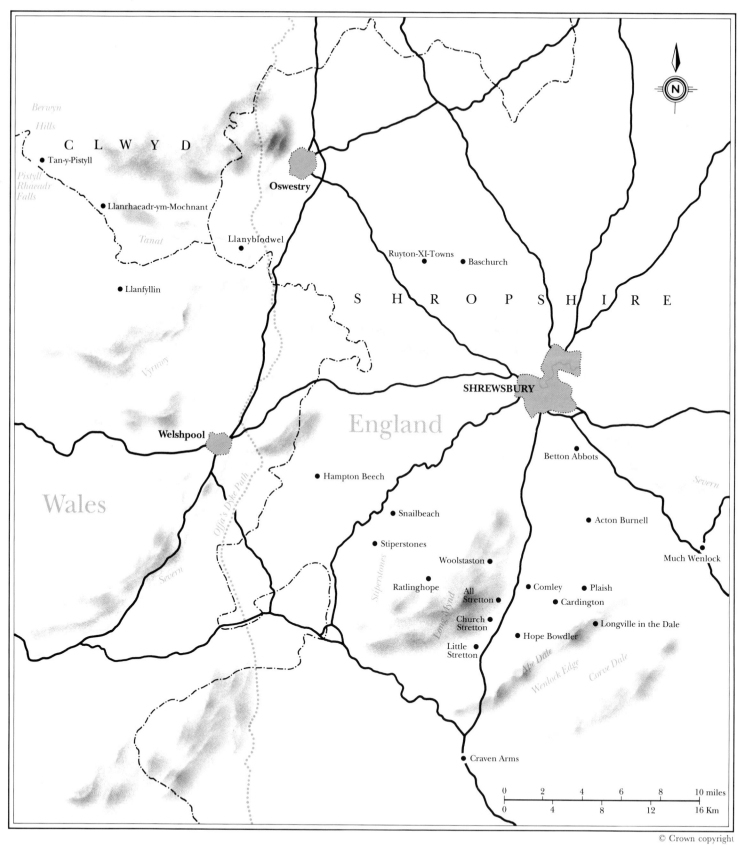

© Crown copyright

4

Shrewsbury and
Wenlock Edge

SHREWSBURY · WENLOCK EDGE · CARADOC HILLS · LONG MYND
STIPERSTONES · MARY WEBB COUNTRY · POWYS CASTLE · WELSHPOOL
BERWYN HILLS · PISTYLL RHAEADR · OSWESTRY

High the vanes of Shrewsbury gleam　　*The flag of morn in conqueror's state*
Islanded in Severn stream,　　*Enters at the English gate:*
The bridges from the steepled crest　　*The vanquished eve, as night prevails,*
Cross the water east and west.　　*Bleeds upon the road to Wales.*

A. E. Housman, *A Shropshire Lad*, No. XXVIII

That is as succinct a picture of the county town of Shropshire as you could wish for. Historically, Shrewsbury was always an island of a town, caught between the politicians and warriors of England and Wales, changing hands both before and after the Norman Conquest, a pawn at one time and a capital piece at another in the long game of Border chess. Geographically, too, the town is an island fortress, caught in a great loop of the River Severn whose neck is less than 300 yards (275 m) across. Small wonder that the Normans began to build a castle here less than a year after they had crossed the Channel, or that they sited it right on the narrowest part of that narrow land bridge. Defended so effectively by its moat of river, and sitting squarely in the fairway between England and Wales, Shrewsbury is a town perfectly placed for both defence and attack, and has seen more than its share of both.

Today's visitor reaps a splendid benefit from this island character of Shrewsbury. The little peninsula jutting into the Severn's loop – technically a 'ness', bulging out as it does into a button-shaped promontory – had been packed full of houses behind the protective shield of the castle by the time that the Border troubles were settled in the seventeenth century. Later developers found no empty spaces to infiltrate, and had to build out and away from the neck of the peninsula. So Shrewsbury's island site is crammed with old buildings and narrow medieval streets. Like superior older brothers and sisters, they smother the gaucheness of the newer members of Shrewsbury's architectural family most effectively, so that one hardly notices the occasional drab 1950s shop front among so much mellow half-timbering and stonework. Shrewsbury suffers as much as any big town from through traffic, but at least one can reflect that the English and Welsh bridges across the Severn are taking away as much traffic as they admit to the cramped old town centre.

Shrewsbury is one of those country towns where people have not lost the custom of nodding and saying 'Good morning' when they catch your eye in the street. This is one of the pleasures of walking around the town; another is the certainty that any set plan to your walk is bound to be subverted, sooner rather than later. You find yourself constantly pulled out of your way by seductive glimpses, half-seen at the far end of a cobbled side lane or over a high wall, of a heavily carved gable end, a cherry tree in blossom, the corner of a hidden church or a convergence of half-timbered houses on some quiet square just off the crowded street. It's handy to take a town plan with you, so that you can navigate yourself back on course after these irresistible side tracks. The island of Shrewsbury is a tangle of history, a delightful labyrinth that shouldn't be hurried through. The walk around the town suggested here is meant only as a framework, to be filled in at your leisure.

The square in the heart of Shrewsbury is as good a place as any to start, by the market hall where Elizabethan builders proudly recorded their names on the wall, along with the day and month that they started work – 15 June – but omitted to mention the year, 1596. That was squeezed in below. With his frock-coated back to the market hall and his plump face looking over High Street stands Clive of India (1725–74) in statue form, green with verdigris. Laden with glory after his military and financial triumphs in India, Robert Clive became Shrewsbury's MP and its mayor, the ordinary boy made spectacularly good. A side track from the main walk route immediately beckons, following the signs behind the market hall up Coffee House Passage to find the Clive House Museum tucked away up a side lane, an exhibition of Georgian life in Shrewsbury, set out in the house where Clive lived during his spell as mayor of the town.

High Street leads to the left from the statue between two magnificent half-timbered buildings, Ireland's Mansion of the 1580s and Owen's Mansion of 1592. Richard Owen had a plaque added to the front of his beautifully carved new house to let all Shrewsbury know that he was a GENTELMAN. Turn from High Street up wide Pride Hill, and stop at the top to look back on a good example of how insensitive building can spoil a classic town view. The old shops and inns slide and curve together down the hill, all of a harmonious piece, to shudder to a halt at a great grey concrete slab of a building at the bottom, over whose bare, square forehead rears an equally bare and square modern red brick clock tower topped with a futuristic spire. At least Dafydd, brother of Prince Llewelyn the Last, was spared that sight in 1283 when he was untied from the sled on which he had been dragged through the jeering crowds lining the streets of Shrewsbury.

Narrow, paved streets, offering glimpses of the town's many churches and lined with buildings that, whatever their outward appearance, are medieval or Tudor in their timber core (OPPOSITE), are quintessential Shrewsbury.

THE XV DAY OF IVNE WAS THIS
BVYLDING BE GONN WILLIAM IONES
AND THOMAS CHARLTON GENT
THEN BAYLIFFES AND WAS ERECTED
AND COVERED IN THEIR TIME

1596

*On the Market Hall in Shrewsbury,
the stone carvers were so anxious to
celebrate the town bailiffs of the
day they forgot to add the year to
the inscription* (ABOVE); *the
dramatically restless black and
white timbering of Ireland's
Mansion* (LEFT), *now one of the
town's many museums, was built
some twenty years before the
Market Hall by Robert Ireland, a
leading merchant in the wool trade
which brought the town its Tudor
wealth.*

Given its key defensive position, Shrewsbury's story was bound to be one of blood and fire. Back in the seventh century it had been known as Pengwern, the seat of the princes of the Welsh kingdom of Powys. The Mercians took it for King Offa at the end of the eighth century, and when the Normans arrived it already had its charter. Llewelyn the Great captured it twice during his drive for power early in the thirteenth century, and Border barons in rebellion against the king made it their stronghold in 1234. Stamping his authority on the region, Edward I not only brought Shrewsbury under his control; he made it his centre of government for this whole region of the Borders while he was crushing the last-ditch revolt of Llewelyn the Last, grandson of Llewelyn the Great.

With his elder brother beheaded after his defeat by Edward in 1283, Dafydd claimed the title of Prince of Wales, and paid for that rash decision with months of misery, hiding in a cave in Snowdonia while the king's men combed the hillsides for him. Dafydd was well aware that any of his followers might betray him at any time, and one of them duly did so. The last truly Welsh Prince of Wales was brought ignominiously to High Cross to be hanged, drawn and quartered, an emphatic full stop to Welsh dreams of autonomy under their own crowned king. Or so the English, safe at Shrewsbury, imagined – until a century later a new flame was ignited along the Borders by the charismatic Owain Glyndŵr.

Harry Hotspur's fiery exchanges with the 'wizard' Glyndŵr make some of the liveliest moments in Shakespeare's *Henry IV Part I*. For all his scorn, though, Hotspur threw in his hand in characteristically wholehearted style with the plan to unseat the usurper Henry Bolingbroke. But in 1403 Hotspur ended up in the same place as Prince Dafydd, hung, drawn and quartered in the same way. Hotspur was luckier, however – he was already dead, having been killed at the Battle of Shrewsbury. Shakespeare has Falstaff claim credit for Hotspur's death with a splendid story of a hand-to-hand fight that lasted an hour by Shrewsbury clock.

Castle Street runs downhill eastwards from High Cross to reach the gates of Shrewsbury Castle. Two side tracks here: the one on the right goes beneath a finely carved square gateway just above the castle, into a cobbled courtyard surrounded by the old half-timbered and brick buildings that house the town's Council Chamber. Almost opposite, on Castle Street, the paved lane of School Gardens runs to the left to the impressively tall and solid stone building where Shrewsbury School was established in the early seventeenth century. 'Hanging' Judge Jeffreys (?1645–89) and Charles Darwin (1809–82) were educated here. A statue of Darwin sits in a handsomely carved chair in front of the old school (now a library), staring pensively out at the dark red sandstone bulk of the castle. You can climb a narrow alleyway of steps known as The Dana to walk a half-circuit under the walls of the castle, ending with a fine view down on to Shrewsbury's railway station – Victorian railway architecture at its best, strikingly gothic but not overblown.

The castle was built and rebuilt over the centuries as the political and military situation dictated. Roger de Montgomery's early Norman walls, parts of which still stand, were comprehensively strengthened by Edward I (1272–1307) in his great drive against the Welsh, and most of what you see today dates from this period. A wide green sward lies in front of the great red stone keep, whose walls are pierced with the windows and doorways added by Thomas Telford (1757–1834) in the 1780s to convert the building into the then Member of Parliament's private residence. Nowadays the keep

The Jacobean gatehouse below the castle, decorated with timber and plaster in the Shrewsbury manner but embellished with a classical pediment, which faces the former meeting place of the Council of the Marches.

houses the museums of several regiments with local connections – the King's Shropshire Light Infantry, the Shropshire Yeomanry and the Shropshire Royal Horse Artillery as well as a display of the Shropshire Lieutenancy. The museum guides are all ex-soldiers, elderly men with straight backs, gentle voices and inextinguishable pride in their occupation. Walking round the display cases of uniforms, weaponry and bravery citations, I learned about the campaign of the Chindit group of behind-the-lines adventurers in Burma during World War II from a quietly spoken man who had been there and done it all. Not a word of his own terrible and stirring experiences passed his lips, however, as he pointed out the mementoes of other brave generations.

From the castle, return up Castle Street to High Cross and turn left along St Mary's Street. It's sad to think that such a historic, lively and important town as Shrewsbury can't drum up a congregation sufficiently large to keep the church of St Mary the Virgin open as a going concern. There are in fact a few services there every year, but St Mary's is officially 'redundant' – which means that a small band of dedicated volunteers keeps the building immaculately clean, and sets out the seating for the concerts and lectures that take place there these days. The church has one treasure above all – its collection of stained-glass windows, the finest in the Borders. They would be reward enough by themselves for a visit to Shrewsbury. You won't see thirteenth-century glass in many churches, but here it fills the heads of four windows in the south wall. The entire east window is of fourteenth-century glass, wonderfully vivid, a Tree of Jesse to rival and perhaps surpass that in St Laurence's at Ludlow. Also of the fourteenth century is the small Crucifixion scene in the south aisle's middle window, with a gentle yet expressive look to all the faces, and Jerusalem mistily portrayed in the background. Don't miss, in the panel opposite, the puffy, oriental faces of the onlookers at the presentation of Christ in the temple; nor, at the west end of the north aisle, the sixteenth-century figure of St John striding along, with hands folded over a bright green robe inside a rich, ruby-red cloak. Another stained-glass masterpiece from St Mary's is the collection of scenes from the life of St Bernard, made for a German abbey in about 1500. With all their formality and stiffness of pose, these works are marvellously expressive of the medieval mind.

St Mary's Street turns into the intriguingly named Dogpole as you descend the hill. Side lanes run off into a maze of medieval roadways hereabouts: Alkmond's Square, where the church of St Alkmond stands opposite a half-timbered house with the legend 'Hold up my goings in thy path' over the door; beyond the church, a heavy-browed old house propped up on posts, from which the steps drop to a lane running away to narrow between two half-timbered houses so close that you could stretch out and drop a love-letter from one bedroom window into the one opposite.

Dogpole meets the steep street called Wyle Cop opposite the Lion Hotel, elegant and comfortable, a Tudor house rebuilt as a coaching inn in the 1770s whose roll of honourable guests includes Dickens and his illustrator Phiz, Jenny Lind, the 'Swedish Nightingale', and Paganini (both performed at the Lion), Thomas de Quincey the opium-eater and William IV when he was Prince of Wales. Below the Lion is Henry Tudor House, whose magnificent half-timbering sheltered Henry Tudor in 1485 on his way to the Battle of Bosworth and the throne.

Carry on down the hill to the bottom, where Wyle Cop runs out level to cross English Bridge, a name to let Border travellers know exactly where they are headed. Shrewsbury's 2 miles (3 km) of river frontage are crossed by eight bridges – road, rail and pedestrian – and from English Bridge on the east round to Welsh Bridge on the west you can enjoy an easy stroll under, over and across them. English Bridge's seven graceful arches carry relief carvings of tritons whose inspiration owes more to Donald Duck than to classical mythology. From here the river-bank path goes under a little bow-girder pedestrian bridge and skirts a bowling green, broadening out through an avenue of lime trees opposite houses on the town side of the Severn with terraced gardens and flights of steps down to landing stages where rowing boats are moored. On the south side of Kingsland toll bridge you see the great red hulk of the present-day Shrewsbury School, which in 1882 took over this superb site, overlooking the Severn, from the town's workhouse; on the north is the Quarry, a public park where stone was dug to build the medieval town walls. Soon the path passes an armless and emasculated statue of Hercules; he was cast in lead in Rome in about 1600, but fell on hard times and had to be rescued from the furnace by the governor of Shrewsbury Gaol after being sold for scrap in 1804.

The Shropshire Horticultural Society wields a good deal of influence in and around Shrewsbury. It was the society who bought the castle in 1921 and gave it to the town, and the following year it presented the lattice-work Porthill Bridge which carries pedestrians across the Severn. A little further on stands Welsh Bridge, much plainer in design than English Bridge, which leads you across the river to an exploration of the district of Frankwell on the southern bank of the Severn. Here you can find the remains of Mardol Quay, once Shrewsbury's busy river port, a maze of pubs, boarding houses, warehouses and docks. Walk under the modern concrete footbridge, suspended asymmetrically from a single post, and on along the river bank round the Severn's sharp curve, looking across to the old and new buildings of the town jumbled together on their rise of ground. Soon a thick band of poplars bisects the arc of the river, shading a host of plants – Himalayan balsam, mugwort and rosebay willowherb among them – thriving on the moisture of the choked old channel hidden in the undergrowth. This was the Barge Gutter, a medieval short cut bringing the clumsy trading barges to the quays, well clear of the fish weir and shallow water in this tight bend of the Severn. It was in use well into the nineteenth century, when floods silted it up.

At the western edge of the Barge Gutter you leave the river and walk back to Welsh Bridge through Frankwell village. The sixteenth-century half-timbered Rowley's House (containing another excellent town museum) stands above Welsh Bridge with its feet in the traffic and its tall gables high overhead, an island of dignity in the island town. It's the final stopping place in this rambling – and by now exhausting – walkabout. Time to restore body and mind in one of the warm old pubs of Shrewsbury, before making for English Bridge and the road south into the Shropshire hills.

A minor road runs due south from the A458, at first through mild-mannered farmland, prosperously easy on the eye. A first taste of the dramatic country ahead comes as you top the rise at Betton Abbots. On the southern horizon stand the tall cones of the Caradoc Hills at the end of the long ridge of Wenlock Edge; further west are the smoothly rolling uplands of the Long Mynd. They call you on through the quiet Shropshire countryside, past Pitchford Hall's black-and-white herringbone walls (the church beside the hall has some fine alabaster memorial engravings of Tudor members of the Ottley family who lived in the great house) to come to Acton Burnell. Here to the left of the road stands the ruined but still impressive castle built by Robert Burnell in

Two of the bridges spanning the Severn, which almost encircles Shrewsbury: the late eighteenth-century Welsh Bridge (LEFT), which replaced the narrow medieval crossing with its great defensive gate tower, and the Porthill suspension bridge (ABOVE), situated between the main English and Welsh road bridges, Victorian in flavour but 1920s in date, and a gift to pedestrians from the Shropshire Horticultural Society.

1284. Burnell was a powerful man, owner of 82 manors in various parts of the country, Lord Chancellor and friend to King Edward I, who became in turn Bishop of Bath and Wells and Bishop of Winchester. It was probably the visit of the king to his wooden castle here in 1283 that prompted Burnell to build a new stronghold, a great rectangular sandstone fortified house whose box of walls, pierced with windows and arches and bounded by corner towers, now encloses a green space from which you can look up to the second and third storeys and the open sky above. Damnably cold and uncomfortable it must have been, and after the Burnell line died out in 1420 the castle was abandoned, later to become a barn.

During his stay here on his final campaign to crush the Welsh and get rid of the pretenders to their crown, Edward I summoned a Parliament which met in a barn near the castle. The two great gable ends which stand 150 feet (46 m) apart in the next field may be the remains of that barn – if so, Parliament had plenty of elbow room while at its business. The church next to the castle dates from the same time and is largely unaltered, the masonry of its arches and windows still so clear cut that they might be faithful Victorian copies. In the north transept is a fine brass of 1382 to Sir Nicholas Burnell, and the superb tomb of Sir Richard Lee, who owned Acton Burnell in late Tudor times. The care taken by the mason over the details of Sir Richard's armour and his wife's dress extended to the individual strands interwoven in the straw mattress on which they lie, and the tiny lap-dog crouching in one of the knight's gauntlets by his side.

From Acton Burnell the road enters a long valley on the west of Wenlock Edge, with conifer-clad hills each side. Bracken, brambles and stunted thorn trees scattered on the hillsides give the valley a remote, moorland feel, enhanced by the knobbled profiles of the Caradoc Hills over the western ridge. At Plaish, sunk deep in the valley, the tall Tudor chimneys of Plaish Hall peep through the trees beside the lane. The house was built by Sir William Leighton, another influential Shropshire gentleman who was a member of the Council of the Marches and Lord Chief Justice of North Wales. The story goes that Sir William, after sentencing a man to death, discovered that he was an expert builder of chimneys. Mindful of his own fine new house still being built – and still chimneyless – Sir William granted the man a stay of execution and set him to work at Plaish. But what did the great judge decide about the fate of his workman once the chimneys were up? Sadly, no-one knows.

Through Longville in the Dale the road goes, to climb the western flank of Wenlock Edge. This long bar of limestone 400 million years old runs north-east from Craven Arms for 16 miles (26 km) to Much Wenlock. Its well-wooded, green face is a focus for the whole of this part of Shropshire – not strikingly upstanding like its western neighbours, but always there to shut off a length of the horizon. Nowhere along the ridge of Wenlock Edge rises even to 1000 feet (300 m), but there are viewpoints all along, all round the compass. Three dales form the counterpoint to the uplifted Edge – Ape Dale to the north-west, Corve Dale to the south-east, and dimpling the spine of the ridge itself the hidden valley of Hopedale. Here stands the stark, fort-like house of Wilderhope Manor, tucked away in the trough of Hopedale in a cut-off position. No roads run near the manor, which stood derelict for many years until the National Trust took it over and leased it to the Youth Hostels Association. Like many big Shropshire houses, it has its ghosts and tales, the best-known of which features its owner in Civil War days, the dashing Major Thomas Sammwood. The major, carrying secret despatches for the king

The gaunt ruins of the gable end of a great barn at Acton Burnell may be all that remains of the meeting place for a Parliament under Edward I, the first to which the Commons were called, which helped seal the fate of Wales.

On Wenlock Edge the wood's in trouble;
His forest fleece the Wrekin heaves *(A.E. Housman)*
and the winds from Shropshire's hills can still buffet the landscape.

and hotly pursued by Roundheads, jumped on his horse from the crag 5 miles (8 km) north that is still known as 'Major's Leap'. The horse was killed in the fall; but Sammwood, landing unscathed in the trees, went on to accomplish his mission on foot.

Wilderhope Manor is a spartan, rather grim place to stay – there was no electricity until 1975 – but as a centre for walks in Hopedale and up to the heights of Wenlock Edge overlooking Ape Dale and Corve Dale the old, tall-chimneyed house is perfect. A quickly finished and rewarding walk is the one that continues along the track behind the manor to turn right over a stile (O.S. ref. 547931), waymarked with a yellow arrow and the buzzard sign of the Shropshire Way long-distance footpath. You cross the stream at the bottom of Hopedale and climb the opposite slope to a dark pine wood on the crest. The view comes quickly up over the slope of the hill – first the domed top of Brown Clee Hill (where you stood at the end of the Ludlow tour), and then the whole width of broad Corve Dale opening below you.

Back in Ape Dale, the B4371 leads west round the base of the Caradoc Hills to come to the snug small town of Church Stretton, lying in a superb position between the Caradocs and the bulging flanks of the Long Mynd. Church Stretton itself is 650 feet (200 m) above sea level, which puts a bracing nip in the breeze blowing along its open streets. But with Caer Caradoc rising to 1505 feet (459 m) on the east, and the towering

Two of the surviving fragments of beautifully expensive late twelfth-century sculpture from the monks' lavatorium, or washing place, in the ruined Cluniac priory at Much Wenlock, situated below Wenlock Edge.

bulk of the Long Mynd reaching almost 1700 feet (520 m) on the west, the impression is of a town cradled deep in the arms of tremendous hills, almost an Alpine feeling. Church Stretton was in fact nicknamed 'Little Switzerland' in the late years of the nineteenth century when mineral springs discovered in the Long Mynd, and the opening of a station on the Shrewsbury–Hereford railway line, gave it the incentive to develop as a spa town. Retired grandees from military and civil service in India loved the landscape, which reminded them of the Punjabi hills they had left behind. The tiny market town grew prosperous, and sprouted a crop of new half-timbered buildings to outshine those that had stood here since medieval days. It also gained a reputation as rather a classy place, a bit snobbish and exclusive, which still clings to it, and not without reason. You will see more well-bred and well-spoken retired gentlefolk perambulating the streets of Church Stretton than almost anywhere else in the Welsh Borders. It's a confident sort of place: the wine bars, boutiques and expensive antique shops tell you that.

One great asset that Church Stretton enjoys is the view from anywhere in the town. Steep hills block the open ends of the streets, real stand-up mini-mountains to the east and west. There are cosy tea shops where you can rest your legs after a day on the hills, and plan more pleasant punishment for the following day, for Church Stretton is a centre for walkers who come to test themselves against these wild uplands. You can set off from anywhere in Church Stretton, or its abutting villages of All Stretton on the north and Little Stretton on the south, and within ten minutes have made your way into valleys as remote as any in the country. The town's small bookshop has a good selection of walking guides to the hills, and you can pick up hints on other routes in conversation around the town. The two walks outlined below are among the most popular, best done out of the summer season when you will have the hills to yourself; for less well-known rambles, refer to the guide books (a good one, obtainable in the bookshop, is Gillian Walker's *The Best Walks in the Shropshire Hills*).

First, the Caradoc Hills. Standing east of Church Stretton, they raise their cones of ancient volcanic rock in a short line from north to south – Caer Caradoc, Willstone Hill and Hope Bowdler Hill. You can walk the whole 3-mile (5-km) range from the hamlet of Comley to the village of Hope Bowdler in a couple of hours, but Caer Caradoc, the tallest at just over 1500 feet (457 m), is the jewel in the crown. There is a fine scramble up to the summit of Caer Caradoc from a muddy track running west from the big old farmhouse at Willstone, 2 miles (3 km) north-east of Church Stretton as the crow flies (and as the walker plods, by way of a track from New House Farm at 466944), but a good 7 miles (11 km) by the road that skirts the hills through Hope Bowdler and Cardington.

From Willstone, follow the track for almost 1 mile (1½ km) to find a stile on your right in a dip (483952). The path mounts a green shoulder over which the head of Caer Caradoc appears, its brow pimpled with outcrops of volcanic rock. A grassy path slants up between them, to bend sharply to the right and reach the summit cairn over which you may spot ravens diving and barking. The grass here is short and soft, making it an ideal place to sit and absorb a tremendous view over the hills and plains of Shropshire and Wales. The Strettons are strung along their flat valley floor to the south-west, beneath the deeply-cut valleys or 'batches' and the smoothly rounded flanks and domed top of the Long Mynd, small enough in area but wild in aspect. Beyond the Long Mynd stand the jagged quartzite outcrops of the Stiperstones, tiny but distinct. In the east, more than twice as far off, the sharp cone of the Wrekin rises out of the Shropshire plain,

Nestling below the Long Mynd, Church Stretton became a fashionable resort in the late nineteenth century, and its spring water is still bottled; modern visitors come to enjoy the walking and exhilarating views.

and further to the east the great 650-foot (200-m) chimney at Buildwas power station sends out a trail of smoke. To the north you look over immensities of low-lying country running away to the borders of Shropshire and beyond. After all this space-gazing, you can foreshorten your view through the Caradoc outliers of The Lawley to the north and Hope Bowdler Hill to the south, and try to make out the shape of the Celtic ramparts that enclose an Iron Age camp on the summit of Caer Caradoc. Legend says that this was where the first-century Celtic chief Caradoc or Caratacus made his last stand after an epic series of retreating battles against the Romans, before being captured, loaded with chains and sent away to Rome and an unknown fate. There may be no connection between Caer Caradoc and its heroic namesake, but up here you can believe what you like.

Tackling the eastern flanks of the Long Mynd by way of Cardingmill Valley is a longer business, but still well within the scope of a reasonably fit walker. Take note, though: weather changes can be remarkably sudden here, and you should equip yourself with warm, waterproof clothing and proper walking boots before you set out – especially in winter, when the well-known and immensely popular beauty spot of Cardingmill Valley will be rid of all its crowds. The valley, steep-sided and winding, burrows into the side of the Long Mynd immediately west of Church Stretton at the end of a well-signposted road, one of a line of 'batches' scored into the eastern flank of the upland mass when the Ice Age snowfield lying on top of the Long Mynd melted and released floodwaters to slice down through the rock. In the early nineteenth century there was a carding mill near the bottom of the valley, smoothing out wool in machines powered by a water wheel. The downrushing water of the valley stream was made for the job, but more sophisticated technology put an end to it.

Above the car park the valley narrows, its steeply slanted sides folding one above another as it bends like a snake and climbs towards the top of the Long Mynd. The track up the valley beside the stream is known as Mott's Road, named after a Church Stretton doctor who raised funds to have the moorland road upgraded so that he could get across the hills to people living far from lowland civilization. There are benches at intervals along the way, and a group of sheep with depraved tastes – their palates have been spoiled by visitors, and are now too finicky for grass and heather shoots; they come up and nuzzle you for sandwiches and titbits, the only hill sheep I have ever met who advance to welcome strangers and suffer themselves to be tickled behind the ears.

Soon the even tighter, narrower and steeper side valley of Lightspout comes down on the left to join the Cardingmill Valley; turn aside from Mott's Road here and climb up under thorn bushes to find the Lightspout waterfall jetting down a bare rock cleft at the top, the stream falling on over a series of steps. Its rustle, splash and rush are the loudest sounds in a deliciously high and lonely spot. A steep scramble up a rocky slide on the right-hand side of the fall leads to a green path climbing by the stream through boggy hollows to reach the bracken-covered back of the Long Mynd. Up here the silence is complete, and the view filled with long, rolling miles of moorland. 'Mynd' is 'Mynydd' in Welsh, meaning a mountain, and this unfrequented high country has a mountainous,

The view westwards from the open, bare, bracken-deep top of the Long Mynd (OPPOSITE) *stretches away over the farmed landscape to the curious twisted shapes of the Stiperstones, the rocky outcrops on the distant ridge.*

windy feel to it. It's the largest area – 10 square miles (26 square km) – of upland grazing country in Shropshire, common land from end to end. There are no trees here, no mountain peaks and few features by which to orientate yourself; 500 yards (450 m) ahead you pick up Mott's Road again and turn to the right back into Cardingmill Valley.

In this 4-mile (6½-km) round walk you put yourself outside and above the everyday world and enter a region both sombre and exhilarating. In fine weather its beauty has an oppressive quality; in winter, as the Reverend Donald Carr found out back in 1865, it can be deadly. *A Night in the Snow*, Mr Carr's objective and detailed account of how he almost died while lost in a snowstorm on the Long Mynd, is still on sale in booklet form in the bookshop at Church Stretton. In the fulsome prose of the day, he tells his terrifying story with all the pace and structure of a novelist. Mr Carr was the rector of Woolstaston, north of Church Stretton on the eastern side of the Long Mynd, and was also responsible for the remote outlying village of Ratlinghope on the west side, 4 miles (6½ km) away from Woolstaston. On 29 January 1865 he set out through the snow on horseback to take the afternoon service at Ratlinghope. The fallen snow was deep enough to force Mr Carr's servant to take the horses back home, but the clergyman went on alone, crawling on hands and knees through the drifts, to reach the lonely village on the moors and take a short service in the company of a handful of people. So far so good, but the journey home was a different matter entirely. Back on the heights, a furious gale had blown up. Mr Carr was at first confident that he was on the right track, but soon realized that he had lost his way, with darkness coming on and the blizzard getting worse all the time. Then he fell down the side of a ravine.

> I found myself shooting at a fearful pace down the side of one of the steep ravines which I had imagined lay far away to my right.... I continued my tremendous glissade head downwards, lying on my back. The pace I was going in this headlong descent must have been very great, yet it seemed to me to occupy a marvellous space of time, long enough for the events of my whole previous life to pass in review before me, as I had often before heard that they did in moments of extreme peril.

He survived that fall, but shortly afterwards, now conscious that he was completely lost, had another even worse, this time losing his hat and gloves. He still had his brandy flask, but 'could hardly get my hands to my mouth for the masses of ice which had formed upon my whiskers, and which were gradually developed into a long crystal beard, hanging half way to my waist'.

Somehow he kept going all through the night, continually falling down and forcing himself up and on again, fighting the overwhelming desire to lie down and drift into sleep. Dawn brought no relief, as a dense fog lay over the Long Mynd. Mr Carr found that he had gone snow blind when he could not tell the front of his watch from the back. Staggering on, he found himself at the top of the Lightspout Valley, and in his weakness tumbled over the upper part of the waterfall – somehow without adding to his injuries. Then he lost his boots:

> They do not seem to have become unlaced, as the laces were firmly knotted, but had burst in the middle, and the whole front of the boot had been stretched out of shape from the strain put upon it whilst laboriously dragging my feet out of deep drifts for

so many hours together, which I can only describe as acting upon the boots like a steam-power boot-jack. And so for hours I walked on in my stockings without inconvenience. Even when I trod upon gorse bushes, I did not feel it, as my feet had become as insensible as my hands.

At last the exhausted man, 'crowned and bearded with ice like a ghastly emblem of winter', stumbled down the Cardingmill Valley and came upon a group of children, who promptly ran away from the apparition. However, help soon came, and Mr Carr made his way home to Woolstaston and eventually to a complete recovery. With this epic adventure in mind, don't attempt the Long Mynd in a blizzard!

A narrow, steep road leaves the B4370 at Church Stretton just south of the entrance to Cardingmill Valley and climbs via Burway Hill and Devil's Mouth to the top of the Long Mynd; after a rough journey between banks of heather it reaches Ratlinghope, where Mr Carr began that terrible homeward journey. Beyond Ratlinghope the road crosses the deep valley of the East Onny River and climbs again, with the rocky profiles of the Stiperstones standing starkly in line astern on the skyline – Shepherd's Rock, Scattered Rock, The Devil's Chair, Manstone Rock and Cranberry Rock. This is the bleakest part of the Shropshire uplands, an area heavy with legend and magical tales that thicken like mist around the harsh outlines of the Stiperstones. They are outcrops of quartzite some 500 million years old, weathered by frost-shattering and ice erosion into weird shapes that dominate their landscape. The Stiperstones ridge holds seams of lead that brought miners to these raw slopes from Roman times until the nineteenth century. The villages under the Stiperstones – Pennerley, Shelve, Snailbeach – still carry the scars of the industry in abandoned shafts, spoil heaps and stagnant pools. The shape of the country hereabouts adds to this atmosphere of bleakness. Deep valleys ('beaches' as opposed to 'batches') cut into the side of the ridge, their slopes far blacker and harsher than anything on the eastern face of the Long Mynd. No wonder that the craggy outlines of the Stiperstones have had such a dark effect on the minds of dwellers in their shadow.

From the car park below the Stones a green path climbs up the slope of the moor, soon becoming a stony track studded with sharp-edged quartzite boulders among which you stumble and slide. Close up, the Stiperstones change shape. Cranberry Rock looks like a section of a battered castle wall. Manstone Rock splits into widely separated sections, some parts squared off by nature as neatly as any mason could manage. Piles of stony clitter lie about the Stones and along the path like carelessly built cairns. There is no easy path on the ridge – the heather, too, is piled with ankle-turning angles of dingy white quartzite. Half an hour's hard going brings you at last to the centrepiece and chief group of the Stiperstones, the Devil's Chair, about whose craggy shape most of the legends are gathered. The Devil was on his way from Ireland, so they say, to fill up Hell Gutter with an apronful of stones when the apron strings slipped and the load fell to earth to form the Chair. When mist gathers over the Stiperstones, the Devil is sitting in his Chair waiting for the Stones to sink into the earth, for that will mean the ruin of England.

On 22 December Wild Edric the Saxon comes to the Stiperstones to meet the other ghosts of Shropshire. Wild Edric, at any rate, has some footing in fact. He was a Mercian thane who burned Shrewsbury in 1069 in a final act of defiance against the new Norman Lords. Legend tells of Wild Edric's marriage to a fairy whom he met while out hunting at

Many dark stories and legends have been woven around the Stiperstones, these weirdly formed outcrops of quartzite sitting high on a ridge which was mined in earlier centuries for its rich seams of lead ore.

the Stiperstones. She agreed to marry him, on condition that he would never mention her sisters. Sure enough, Edric mentioned them in the end, and his fairy wife disappeared, leaving him to die of a broken heart. He lies deep in an abandoned lead mine near Snailbeach, ready to return to the lands he forfeited to the Normans on the day when a Saxon king shall sit again on the throne of England.

The Devil's Chair is a fitting place to pay tribute to the Shropshire writer Mary Webb (1881–1927), who knew all the legends of the Stiperstones and wove their brooding, baneful presence into several of her novels. 'So the throne stood,' she wrote of the Devil's Chair in *The Golden Arrow*:

> blank, massive, untenanted, yet with a well-worn air. It had the look of a chair from which the occupant had just risen, to which he will shortly return ... Nothing ever altered its look. It remained inviolable, taciturn, evil. It glowered darkly on the dawn;

Shelve, like other villages below the Stiperstones, still bears the scars of its lead-mining history in the shape of ruined engine houses and deserted shafts.

it came through the snow like jagged bones through flesh . . . For miles around, in the plains, the valleys, the mountain dwellings it was feared.

Mary Webb brought the Shropshire landscape vividly to life, poetically yet with complete honesty, in five novels written during and after World War I – *The Golden Arrow*, *Gone to Earth*, *The House in Dormer Forest*, *Seven for a Secret* and *Precious Bane*. She was fully alive to the dark and threatening side of Shropshire, using it to colour such places as 'Undern Hall' (Wilderhope Manor) in *Gone to Earth*, 'Dormer Valley' (Hope Valley, west of the Stiperstones) in *The House in Dormer Forest*, and 'Sarn Mere' (a mixture of local pools, including Ellesmere and Bomere) in *Precious Bane*. Local people still read her work, and prize their early editions, but, as in her lifetime, Mary Webb doesn't really sell. She had a sad, intense life. Her mother was a strange, reclusive individual with whom Mary never had a close relationship; she adored her father and went into a long mourning period after his death. She suffered from the disfiguring thyroid disorder of Graves' Disease, and became sensitive about her pinched face and protuberant eyes, caused by the illness. She gradually became estranged from her husband, a teacher, and was desperately unhappy whenever his job took them away from Shropshire. When she died at 46, she still had not established her name as a writer, though shortly afterwards the praise of Stanley Baldwin, then Prime Minister, brought her posthumous fame. *Precious Bane* and *Gone to Earth* are still in print, and give an excellent idea of the power with which she evoked her beloved Shropshire.

Beyond the Devil's Chair the ridge path goes on to reach the two outliers of the Stiperstones, Scattered Rock and Shepherd's Rock. Returning to the car park, you continue along the road under the western flank of the Stiperstones, where local people come in their lunch hour to park their cars and enjoy the view as a relish to their sandwiches. Tall brick chimneys and the ivy-smothered ruins of engine-houses stand in dingles below the road, remnants of the now vanished lead-mining industry. Above Stiperstones village, Mytton Dingle carves deep into the side of the ridge between the towering black sides of Perkins Beach and Oak Hill, as brooding a backdrop as any in Mary Webb's books. On the northern outskirts of Snailbeach lies a bald grey mound of mining spoil, the last grim farewell to the Stiperstones.

Now you turn off to cross the wide valley of the Rea Brook on the B4499. Ahead the horizon is filled by the green back of Long Mountain. Turn right on to the B4386 at Brockton, and immediately left to find a winding lane climbing into the hidden valleys of Long Mountain. The lane slides and snakes in and out of wooded dells, through hamlets like Hampton Beech where the houses cling to the hillsides like leeches, high above lonely farms facing down lovely valleys, on and up to cross the Welsh Border and turn left along the old Roman road running down the crest of the range. The road, as straight as every Roman road should be, connected the settlement of Viriconium at Wroxeter with the fort of Lavrobrinta at Forden Gaer, south of Welshpool. The rolling highlands of the Berwyn Hills lie dead ahead as you turn right for Welshpool and Powis Castle.

After the small and ruinous castles that pepper the whole length of the Borders, it comes as a treat to find a really gigantic castle complete and in good repair, lording it over the landscape with the arrogance of red-faced Powis Castle on a great mound in the middle of its great park. Castell Coch is the Welsh name for it, 'the Red Castle', a tremendous dusky sandstone pile whose core was built in about 1250 by the last Prince of Powys, Owain ap Gruffydd, before he bowed to the inevitable and renounced all Welsh claims to sovereignty at Shrewsbury. Encasing that structure is the building one sees today, dating from the early fourteenth century. Powis Castle was never besieged and captured by any Marcher Lord, since the princes of Powys were well in with the English; but during the Civil War it underwent and capitulated to a Roundhead siege. In the centre of the great courtyard prances the statue of a winged horse, a half-naked goddess on his back blowing a trumpet to the sky in wild abandon. The grounds were laid out in the eighteenth century by Lancelot 'Capability' Brown, and there are several walks, long and short, among the magnificent collection of trees.

Welshpool lies along the A483 from Powis Castle, surrounded by ranges of hills, each with its own particular shape. To the north-east the sharp volcanic peaks of the Breidden Hills stand high above the valley of the Severn, while further east and south stretches the long green ridge of Long Mountain. On the west rise the foothills of the Berwyn Hills, rolling away into Wales with their flanking valleys and rounded tops in shapes reminiscent of the Long Mynd. In spite of this superb cradle of hills, Welshpool

The once-forbidding exterior of Powis Castle, near Welshpool, was softened after the Restoration, with new windows which lit grand staircases and rich interiors, the embellishment of sculpture (ABOVE), and with the construction of terraced gardens stepping down the dramatic escarpment on which the castle stands (RIGHT). In one wing of the castle the jewels and treasures which Robert Clive brought back as his booty from India are now imaginatively displayed.

looks, feels and speaks English. When the princes of Powys held sway in Powis Castle the town, then known simply as 'Pool', was the capital of the kingdom of Powys, but Border history drew it firmly under English influence. The passing centuries have had their way with Welshpool's architecture, too, so that these days you find every building style from early and late medieval – when the town prospered through wool-trading, sheep sales and flannel-making – to solid Georgian, overblown Victorian and flat-featured modern. This diversity of appearance gives Welshpool a jumbled and homely atmosphere, a market town with odd corners and quirks in a small compass. The church of St Mary the Virgin stands high above all this, with an ancient, rough-hewn tub of solid stone opposite its south door. Some say the stone, known as Maen Llog, was once a druidical altar slab.

Walking from St Mary's along Church Street, you pass a big red-brick warehouse with an inscription all round its top, 'J. & M. Morris Agricultural Implement Depot', a fine example of Victorian business building. On the corner where Church Street joins Broad Street is one of those small pleasures of a walk round Welshpool – a plaque on the wall of an unremarkable house, stating that it was built in 1692 by Gilbert and Ann Jones, 'whose ancestor Roger Jones, *TEMP.* Edward VI, is reputed to have been the first Welsh Jones, and paid to the Lord of Powys, the Feudal Due of a Peppercorn at Midsummer'. This house makes a connection with our earlier Ludlow tour, for here in the eighteenth century lived the grandfather and father of Robert Owen (see p. 103), the Newtown boy who put into practice his dreams of a better life for working people.

The best way to get the feel of Welshpool is to walk from Church Street up the wide sweep of Broad Street, from which those side alleys so characteristic of Welsh Border towns run off into the shadows. One by one the pieces of Welshpool history slot into place. You pass the heavy Victorian town hall, built in 1879, complete with the inevitable looming clock tower, whose face is lit in lurid green by night. All activity in Welshpool centres on the upper floor of the town hall – magistrates' court sessions, dances, lectures, exhibitions – while in a big open space below, the town's market is still held. Above the town hall, where Broad Street becomes High Street, stands the half-timbered Pheasant Inn, opposite a small but imaginative art gallery – how many country towns can boast one of those? – and the dimity charm of the ornate black-and-white Buttery tea rooms. These are followed by a hulking, mid-Victorian Methodist church, the little old Mermaid Inn propped up between a health food shop and a ladies' hair stylist, and the dark-beamed Talbot Inn with black-shuttered windows from which the mid-afternoon drinkers peer furtively out. Here High Street climbs seamlessly into Mount Street while the procession of shoulder-to-shoulder buildings continues: old cottages, a Bethel chapel and the Green Dragon Inn where the road tops out and the town comes to a halt.

Driving out of Welshpool by this route along the A490 you encounter views across the wide valley of the River Vyrnwy, enfolded by tall hills; the sense of being well and truly into Wales is reinforced by the multi-syllabic names on the signposts. The A490 crosses the river and runs on westward, to dip down on the outskirts of Llanfyllin past the old workhouse of Y Dolydd, a great complex handsomely but grimly built in dark

The flat plain of the Vyrnwy, which joins the Severn at the English border, near Offa's Dyke to the north of Welshpool (OPPOSITE).

stone in 1838 under the Poor Law statutes. Llanfyllin Union comprised 19 parishes, and 250 paupers were collected here from all over the area to serve out the life sentences of hard work and separation from their loved ones imposed on them for the crime of poverty.

The little town of Llanfyllin straggles in one main street along the road. The Cain Valley Hotel stands sturdily in the centre opposite the tiny town square where Welsh gossip goes on behind the steamy windows of the little café. There's a pungent smell of dung in the streets, and a clutch of old-fashioned shops. There were tanneries, brickworks and maltings in Llanfyllin back in the eighteenth and nineteenth centuries, but these days it's a quiet little place. Llanfyllin bricks built the classically-styled church in 1704; the various benefactors who contributed funds to the building are recorded along the big gallery at the west end of the church, including 'Seaven hundred and Thirty Pounds' given by 'Her Moft Gracious and Glorious Majesty Queen Anne'.

The elderly church caretaker stood with me looking at the stained-glass windows and reminiscing about the Dugdale family who gave them. She could remember when the Dugdales lived in state at the big house of Llwyn, pulled down not long ago when the family left Llanfyllin. Welsh as a language is not as common in the area as it once was. 'My mother was fluent Welsh. But an English lady moved in next door, and wouldn't speak Welsh to her little boy. So my mother thought *she* wouldn't speak it to us, either. Now I regret that – I wish I had more Welsh. The young people are beginning to take it up again, though.'

A polite request in the shop of Jones, Chemist and Druggist, will admit you to an upstairs room containing one of Llanfyllin's hidden treasures. The entire room was painted with murals in 1812 by the French prisoner-of-war Captain Pierre Augerand during his time of captivity on parole in Llanfyllin. Captain Augerand was one of a couple of hundred such prisoners, most of them wounded in one way or another, who had given their word not to stray more than a mile ($1\frac{1}{2}$ km) from the town. On one occasion, wanting to go to a dance being held just outside the allotted area, the prisoners dug up the boundary marker and carried it before them to the ball so as to be able to say they had kept within bounds. Pierre Augerand only had a mixture of crushed slate and sheep dip to paint with, and in this primitive medium he created primitive images of rocky archways and waterfalls, towering mountains and islands, all in sombre tints of blue, grey and black. What an experienced psychologist would make of these claustrophobic paintings I don't know, but the message of repression conveyed by the gloomy colours, escapist fantasy and phallic shapes is clear enough. There is a happy ending to the story, though. From the window the Frenchman watched and fell in love with the daughter of the rector of Llanfyllin, and after his release returned to the town to find and marry her.

From Llanfyllin, the B4391 and B4580 take you north into the eastern flanks of the Berwyn Hills. This is an area still little visited by tourists, with few villages and fewer roads. The Berwyns are rounded hills of Silurian rock – mudstone, sandstone and shale – smoothed by Ice Age erosion. Up to these heights the local farmers used to drive their sheep and cattle to summer pasture, staying for months at a time in huts known as *hafodydd* ('summer dwellings') – the name can still be found attached to remote upland farms. This is country for map and compass, knapsack and boots, where you can walk for hours on rough tracks and sheep paths, seeing nobody. At the eastern edge of the

Berwyns lies the village of Llanrhaeadr-ym-Mochnant, 'the church by the falls of the stream where the pigs are found'. Llanrhaeadr in its remote position is a backwoods kind of place, where hill farmers bring sheep for sale and fill up their cars with goods from the village's few shops. Its importance in local life is shown by its possession of three inns, in each of which you can hear all the farming and social gossip you could wish.

The village has a wider importance to Welsh cultural life, however, for it was here that William Morgan (1545–1604) translated the Bible into Welsh after taking up the living as vicar in 1578. The Welsh Bible, published in 1588, had an enormous effect among Welshmen whose language had been in decline for 50 years, ever since the Acts of Union of the early years of the Reformation. With no Bible available that they could understand, Welsh speakers in many regions had abandoned Christianity altogether. Now they had a rallying point for language, culture, faith and national spirit. The 'Bishop Bible' – Morgan had been appointed Bishop of St Asaph by the time his work appeared in print – revitalized Welsh pride in Welsh heritage, though it did little for the translator in material terms. He made no money out of his long-drawn-out endeavour, and died in 1604 with just £110 to his name.

Another writer well known in Wales, George Borrow (1803–81), came to Llanrhaeadr-ym-Mochnant in 1854 while researching *Wild Wales*, staying at the Wynnstay Arms, which he found large but not very cheerful. Borrow was on his way to see one of the Seven Wonders of Wales, the great waterfall of Pistyll Rhaeadr at the upper end of the valley. A winding lane runs up the valley of the River Disgynfa for 4 miles ($6\frac{1}{2}$ km) under high, rocky hillsides, past farms and cottages dotted along the way. The valley narrows and steepens, leading to bluffs of bare rock overhanging the waterfall, which you can see from some distance pouring in long skeins of white water over its rim of hard felsite rock and down the cliff face. A line of larches stands against the sky, sloping down to the top of Pistyll Rhaeadr, and more larches and pine trees fill the head of the valley around the fall, a dramatic and lovely scene.

A path drops from the café of Tan-y-Pistyll, discreetly converted from an old stone building, down to a narrow footbridge directly below the falls. Pistyll Rhaeadr is a more than popular place for visits and picnics in summer, but at any time of year the sheer size and power of those crashing sheets of water overpowers all beholders. From the upper rim 240 feet (75 m) above you the water plunges in a straight fall of well over 100 feet (30 m), jumping into space from ledges in the cliff face to shower down into a natural rock pool. From here it gushes out again under an arch of rock to tumble down below the footbridge into a quiet pool. Drifts of spray jet out of the rock arch, and a cold blast of air gusts across the bridge. The noise of the fall is stupendous – a background rush and roar from the upper fall, overlaid with the crash of the lower spout foaming out of the rock arch and the deeper bubbling note of the river as it jets over the final step into the bowl below the bridge. The whole rock niche seems to shudder and vibrate with the thud of falling water. This is one of those rare natural wonders that lives up to all expectations – a literally stunning sight and sound. 'What shall I liken it to?' mused George Borrow. 'I scarcely know, unless to an immense skein of silk agitated and disturbed by tempestuous blasts, or to the long tail of a grey courser at furious speed.'

After viewing the falls, Borrow went to the nearby farmhouse to inspect the inscriptions and verses in the visitors' book. Typically, he seized the opportunity to show off his knowledge of Welsh, in fact rather shaky.

The thundering falls of Pistyll Rhaeadr, one of the Seven Wonders of Wales, where the water's main hundred-foot leap in what George Borrow described as 'thin beautiful threads' has always entranced and frightened spectators.

Among these compositions was a Welsh *englyn* on the Rhyadr, which though incorrect in its prosody I thought stirring and grand. I copied it, and subjoin it with a translation which I made on the spot.

Crychiawg, ewynawg anian-yw y Rhyadr
Yn rhuo mal taran;
Colofn o dwr, gloyw-dwr glan,
Gorwyllt, un lliw ag arian.

Foaming and frothing from mountainous height,
Roaring like thunder the Rhyadr falls;
Though its silvery splendour the eye may delight,
Its fury the heart of the bravest appals.

Back at Llanrhaeadr-ym-Mochnant, follow the B4580 and B4396 eastwards down the valley of the River Tanat with hills on either side. Some rise in ridge shape; others are conical, like the green hump beside the road crowned with the hill fort of Llwyn Bryn Dinas. Half-way along the flat floor of the valley you cross back into Shropshire. Just short of the junction of the B4396 with the A495, take a side lane to the right to find the secluded little village of Llanyblodwel. By the three-arched bridge over the wide and shallow River Tanat stands the fourteenth-century Horseshoe Inn. Of all the bent and creaky old half-timbered inns in the Welsh Borders, the Horseshoe must rate among the bentest and creakiest; a black-and-white picture of rural charm where you can buy a day permit to fish for trout and grayling along the inn's stretch of the Tanat. The fishing is free if you are staying at the Horseshoe (open to guests between March and September); try to avoid splitting your head open on the forest of china mugs hanging from the low ceiling beams.

An octagonal tower of curious design rises above the trees beyond the river. It belongs to the church of St Michael the Archangel, one of the most eccentric essays in Victorian Gothic you are ever likely to see. The key is kept at Llan Farm behind the Horseshoe Inn. 'It's not exactly a lovely church,' said the occupant of Llan Farm as he handed me the key, 'but it's *interesting*. The vicar was a muscular Christian, who over-gothicized it.' That was an understatement. I burst out laughing when I opened the door to be slapped in the face with an exotic riot of exuberant decoration. The Reverend John Parker, vicar of Llanyblodwel from 1845 to 1860, had an excess of energy and zeal which he poured out – along with a reputed £10,000 – in an all-out attack on the church. 'From Lightning & Tempest, from Earthquake & Fire, Good Lord Deliver Us' runs the inscription over the archway connecting tower to church, and some of his more aesthetically-minded parishioners may have found their tongues in their cheeks when reading that. The entire interior of the church is filled with lightning and tempest, earthquake and fire in the form of lettered texts, ceiling decorations, lettered and painted archways and window frames, an elaborate wooden choir loft on stone pillars, red and blue paint and gold leaf everywhere; enough ranks of pews to seat an army; soaring tower and gabled clerestory windows. The whole church is a wild, overpowering feast of gothic elaboration, that is nevertheless disarming in its sincerity and whole-heartedness. No-one visiting St Michael's could be in any doubt about the strength of Mr Parker's faith, let alone the power of his personality.

There's a good, strong echo of gothic, too, in the architecture of the old village school (now a house) as you leave Llanyblodwel to rejoin the A495. At the White Lion Inn, turn left on the A483 to reach Oswestry 3 miles (5 km) to the north. To your left are the Border hills, and to your right the broad, marshy flatlands of the north Shropshire plain. Oswestry stands guard over this transition of landscapes between Wales and England, a town with a foot in both camps. In fact, when the FitzAlan lords ruled the area in Norman times, Oswestry was virtually their private kingdom, unattached to either country. Norman armies sallied out west from their base in Oswestry Castle to subdue the Welsh princes who had been fatally weakened by their own internecine squabbles.

The castle mound, now a public garden, stands tall in the centre of Oswestry, with steep little pathways leading to two big lumps of masonry on the flat top, all that remains of the Norman castle. From here there is a grand view over the whole town – Victorian brick terraces to the north, with the enormous 40-acre (16-ha) Iron Age fort of Old Oswestry looming beyond; the old town centre to the south, its curving streets partly hidden by the grey bulk of the Guildhall. Oswestry grew as best it could under the rather ineffective protection of the castle. It was burned by the English in 1216 and the Welsh in 1234. Owain Glyndŵr carried on with the damage in 1400, and during the 1540s five catastrophic fires cut a swathe through the centre. The Roundheads destroyed the castle in 1644, and battered most of St Oswald's church to pieces for good measure. Such were the penalties of being a Border town.

Climb down from the castle mound and walk into the market square, Bailey Head, where on market days the stalls line up on the sloping ground and Oswestry people wander up for a chat and half a pound of carrots. The covered Powis Hall Market at the top of the square is a big, cheerful shed of a place with a ramp leading to an upper gallery of small shops selling carpets, sweets, brassware, flowers, ladies' macs and coats. Bailey Street, a pedestrian thoroughfare, leads down from the market square into the bustle of the town, meeting Cross Street by Llwyd Mansion, an unornamented but dignified old half-timbered building of 1604 standing among the best and worst that the succeeding centuries could manage in the way of architecture.

Church Street is a pleasure to wander down, running south out of Oswestry, a mish-mash of the town's centuries of development. Here stands the little old Fox Inn, with a black-and-white frontage rather younger than its back regions where brick walls bulge between gnarled black timbers. Well-worn shops and pubs line the street, which goes south past the church of St Oswald, destroyed by the troops of Parliament. They stabled their horses in the ruins, feeding them out of the ancient parish chest filled with corn. The interior of St Oswald's is enormously wide, so that the roof, which would look tall enough in a village church, seems oppressively low here. The great tower is Norman – it escaped the Civil War destruction – and looks across the churchyard to the big half-timbered gable of Oswestry's old school, built just after 1400.

On the southern edge of town are two pieces of Oswestry history not to be missed. Church Street becomes Pool Street, and here on the right Croeswylan Lane runs down

*Abandoned after the Romans conquered Britain, the huge Iron Age hill fort of Old Oswestry, Yr Hên Ddinas (*OPPOSITE*), guarded the Welsh border as firmly as did the new fortifications of Oswestry after the Norman Conquest.*

Llwyd Mansion, dated 1604, is Oswestry's prime example of the half-timbering which is a hallmark of the border country. Defence was the other feature, and Bailey Street records the site of the Norman castle earthwork.

the side of Oswestry's secondary school. Set in the wall of the school grounds at the junction of Pool Street and Croeswylan Lane is the Croeswylan Stone, large and pillow-shaped, with a hollow in the middle. It was the base of a medieval 'weeping cross' or place of penance that stood nearby, where in the plague year of 1559 the country people with market goods came to sell them without having to enter the stricken town. Legend says that they washed the money they took in the hollow of the stone, in the vain hope of cleansing it of the plague. Almost opposite Croeswylan Lane is Weston Lane, which runs south-west to pass the big brick house of Plas Wilmot behind its tall garden walls. This was the birthplace of Wilfred Owen (1893–1918), the delicate Shropshire boy who in such poems as 'Dulce et Decorum Est', 'Mental Cases' and 'Spring Offensive' found a voice which expressed more clearly than any other the horrors of the trenches of World War I. Invalided out in 1917, Owen met another great war poet, Siegfried Sassoon, while

Set among the quality food shops which are characteristic of all these border towns,
the last vestige of the one-time defences of Oswestry is the site of the gate that was
the principal passageway through the stout walls.

in a convalescent hospital in Scotland, and was fired to produce some of his greatest poetry. He returned to France, won the Military Cross for capturing a German machine gun and scores of prisoners, and was killed one week before the end of the war.

The A5 will speed you from Oswestry straight back to Shrewsbury, but take the time to turn off along the B4397 into the gently billowing farmland of the Shropshire plain. This is an unsung, unfrequented part of the Borders, much of which was a great marshy morass until eighteenth-century drainage reclaimed it for agriculture. Two miles (3 km) along the road you pass through the intriguingly-named village of Ruyton-XI-Towns, laid out at the start of the fourteenth century by Edmund FitzAlan, Earl of Arundel, as a market town from which he hoped to increase his revenues. He incorporated eleven tiny townships into the new development – Eardiston and West Felton, Wykey and Coton, Haughton, Rednal, Shelvock and Sutton, Tedsmore,

Shottaton and Ruyton itself. Some of these names can still be found on the map, hamlets these days. But Ruyton-XI-Towns never amounted to much as a market centre – the whole area was too unsettled, and after Owain Glyndŵr's rebellion Ruyton was incorporated for a time in the Welsh princedom of Powys, denying it traffic with the English side of the border. Shrewsbury and Oswestry proved too powerful a pair of rivals. Ruyton declined to the status of a village, a quiet place today where from the castle mound by the church, with its couple of stubs of castle wall, there is a wide view over the shallow valley to the big modern dairy on the outskirts of the village which keeps Ruyton busy nowadays.

Two miles (3 km) further along the B4397, turn left in the centre of Baschurch village to find one of the most historic sites in the Borders and a fitting place to end this tour. Standing alone in the fields north of the village is an earthwork shaped like an ampersand (&). A flat lower ring is surmounted by a central mound with a flat, grassy top where rabbits burrow in the loose soil. To the east two embankments run away from the lower mound, one south-east to peter out on the edge of a tree-fringed pool, the other north-east to end in a small circular earthwork. This strange configuration in the countryside is The Berth. It was probably built as a fort during the Iron Age, utilizing one of the drumlins or knolls left behind when the melting ice scoured the landscape at the end of the last Ice Age. Quite why it took the shape it did remains a mystery.

Further mystery surrounds its subsequent history, for tradition says that The Berth, not Shrewsbury, was the site of Pengwern, the capital of the princedom of Powys during the Dark Ages and the seat of its court. In Welsh poetry the story is told of Prince Cynddylan the Brave, who was killed *c.*640 defending Pengwern against the English in a great battle in the marshes. His body was brought for burial to Eglysau Basa – 'the church at Baschurch'? – to be buried. There are strong links with the Arthurian legend: the heroic king defending a kingdom on the brink of defeat by alien forces; his death in battle among marshes and meres; his body taken away by faithful followers to a holy place of safety. How deeply the tradition of The Berth is rooted in fact can't be unravelled. Certainly Pengwern was sacked in the seventh century, and a bronze cauldron of the sixth century has been unearthed at The Berth. Whether fact or fancy, though, The Berth is a good place to linger, looking out on the rolling plain and musing on the dark corners of Border history, before turning south again for Shrewsbury.

The parish church of Baschurch, with its thirteenth-century west tower, stands amid a scattered settlement typical of this part of Shropshire, where generations of settlers cleared the woodlands and drained the lakes.

5

From Llangollen to the Vale of Clywd

LLANGOLLEN · RUABON · MALPAS · MOLD · FLINT · HALKYN MOUNTAIN
HOLYWELL · MOSTYN DOCKS · VALE OF CLWYD AND CLWYDIAN HILLS
DENBIGH · RUTHIN · CASTELL DINAS BRAN

If any town has cause to be grateful for the landscape in which it is set, that town is Llangollen. The Vale of Llangollen is impressively beautiful seen from any point of the compass, but the best effect accumulates slowly as you drive west up the valley along the A5 from Oswestry. The gentle, rolling countryside of the Shropshire and Cheshire border shrugs off its dulcet charms and heaves mountainous shoulders skywards. The River Dee carves its way from west to east over a rock bed of shale and slate, the outlying foot of the Berwyn Hills which loom to the south. The river runs as a boundary between those old Silurian foundations and more recent beds of limestone and sandstone on the north, standing in long, bare ledges high over the Vale of Llangollen. So the effect as you venture westward is of high crags on your right, high green hills with rounded brows and wooded slopes on your left, climbing more and more steeply to enfold the little town of Llangollen where the two opposing valley sides close up. Roads, river, a disused railway and a well-used canal all squeeze up the Dee's valley to Llangollen, but the eye is continually drawn up and away to the tops of the hills and crags. One in particular dominates the view from down on the valley floor at Llangollen – the round-sided, flat-topped knoll of Castell Dinas Bran which sits right in the throat of the Eglwyseg valley that winds due north from the town under the limestone escarpment. The exposed bands of limestone, known as Creigiau Eglwyseg, are the result of a gigantic horizontal landslip along the fault that divides the older and younger rocks of the Vale of Llangollen. The knoll of Castell Dinas Bran, facing the limestone cliffs only a short distance away, belongs to the southern Silurian range, a great knob of ancient shale left alone to sit in smoothly grassy contrast to its hard-faced young neighbours, crowned with the ruins of a thirteenth-century stronghold of Welsh princes; through its shattered arches you can see tiny points of bright sky as you stand 1000 feet (305 m) below in the streets of Llangollen. The broken remains of Castell Dinas Bran are

The bridge over the Dee in the centre of Llangollen, carrying Thomas Telford's great road which brought the waves of tourists early in the nineteenth century to admire the impressive beauty of the Vale of Llangollen.

an aiming point for eyes everywhere around Llangollen, a truly dramatic guardian of the little town in the valley.

Llangollen has an entirely Welsh feel to it, with these days a strong dash of internationalism for spice. Every year in the second week of July the town plays host to thousands of singers, dancers and musicians from all over the world at its International Eisteddfod. This is an event quite different in character from the Welsh *eisteddfodau*. The idea, born in 1947 when all nations of the world were bruised and broken by war, is not to uphold one particular cultural tradition, but to mingle as many as possible, in hopes of increased understanding and respect between performers and onlookers. It works, too. There's an irresistible energy about the town in that week in July, the streets filled with national music, dance, costumes and chatter from the Andes to the Carpathians by way of Lesotho, Singapore and the Rhondda Valley. Llangollen has a European Centre for Folk Studies, too, offering courses, language training, exhibitions and performances based round any and every aspect of European traditional culture. The International Eisteddfod gave rise to the Centre, and Llangollen has been wonderfully enriched by both.

Nearly 200 years before any of these high-minded matters was ever dreamed of, the little slate-quarrying and market town had had its isolation broken by eighteenth-century seekers after Romantic Crags and Aweful Chasms. In the Vale of Llangollen they found what they yearned for – crags and mountains, slopes and dells, a wide river foaming over rapids and a snug little town set on both sides of an ancient bridge. The weavers, farmers and quarrymen of Llangollen were happy enough to see the new money pour in, and the town became an immensely popular centre for exploring the Berwyns, the Clwydian Hills to the north and the higher ranges further west into Wales. When Thomas Telford improved what is now the A5 road through the Vale of Llangollen in the 1820s (the main London–Holyhead coaching route passed through the town) the visitors came in ever greater numbers. And they still do, to walk in the hills, fish for salmon in the Dee, cruise the canal in horse-drawn boats and loiter along the streets and the riverside paths. Llangollen has a number of big old hotels – the Royal (an excellent, comfortable and friendly place by the bridge), the Hand, the Wynnstay, Benson's, the Bull Inn with 'stabling' advertised on its tiled name-board. Like Presteigne, the town has the atmosphere of a place that has seen centuries of through traffic, a linear tendency in its street-plan that draws you effortlessly on as you explore.

Starting at the car park on Market Street (*Heol y Farchnad* – most Llangollen street nameplates are bilingual) walk down East Street past the old school which houses the European Centre for Folk Studies, and on to Victoria Promenade beside the Dee which rushes east over flat slabs of dark shale towards the massive arches and sharply angled buttresses of the bridge. The old corn mill by the bridge is built of great rough chunks of raw slate, the gaps in its walls filled in with broken pieces of millstone. There's a cluttered junk shop in the mill, well worth picking over, and on the other side of the lane an enormous old loom which wove textiles until very recently. As a thriving holiday town Llangollen is adept at these conversions – mill into junk shop, school into cultural centre, another school into a health centre: signs of a town with a healthy, positive attitude to its past, present and future.

From the bridge you look down on Llangollen's railway station, closed to the travelling public these days and lovingly refurbished as the headquarters of the Flint and

Llangollen's railway station below the old road bridge, closed to potential travellers by the axe which Dr Beeching wielded in the early 1960s, now houses lovingly restored steam trains.

Deeside Railway Preservation Society. The big green locomotives and chocolate-and-cream carriages stand by the immaculately clean platforms and buildings, emanating a romance whose spirit those eighteenth-century visitors to Llangollen would have recognized, though they never would have associated it with railways. The trail leads up a steep bank on the north side of the Dee, at the top of which the Llangollen Canal curves past its old wharf, crane and stables. Horse-drawn narrow-boats go up and down the waterway from here, a tremendous attraction in summer. This section of the canal was not meant to be a commercial route when it was planned at the turn of the nineteenth century; it was intended as a channel to feed water from the Dee to the Ellesmere Canal at Pont-Cysyllte 5 miles (8 km) down the valley – of which more later. But a canal it became, and after an unsuccessful commercial life it flourished as a leisure attraction. There is a fine view from the wharf over the town's slate roofs and untidy but pleasing

The straight-sided banks of the Llangollen Canal, which once carried freight and now carries many pleasure boats, and was originally intended as a simple water channel connecting the River Dee to the Ellesmere Canal.

jumble of several centuries of architecture – tall cottages that predate Llangollen's tourist boom, big hotels, fine large Victorian houses on the hill slopes and terraces of bright red bricks manufactured at nearby Ruabon, an eye-catching feature throughout the town.

George Borrow chose Llangollen as his first base when he came to Wales in 1854 to write *Wild Wales*. He settled with his wife and step-daughter in lodgings in this part of the town, north of the river, and set out from here on his mighty walk-and-talk explorations all over the surrounding hills, usually accompanied by the even-tempered and willing Llangollen weaver John Jones. Borrow tells an entertaining story of the miserable black cat that befriended him, 'mere skin and bone ... with an eruptive malady and a bronchitic cough'. The poor brute had belonged to a previous vicar of Llangollen, and had been driven out of the vicarage by the new incumbent's own cats and dogs. Nine out of ten inhabitants of this north bank area of the town were Dissenters, and the wretched cat, a Church of England animal, was victim of persecution savage enough to qualify it for feline canonization, as Borrow recounts:

> If the workmen of the flannel factory, all of whom were Calvinistic Methodists, chanced to get a glimpse of it in the road from the windows of the building, they would sally forth in a body, and with sticks, stones or for want of other weapons, with clots of horse-dung, of which there was always plenty on the road, would chase it up the high bank.

The Borrows' landlady, 'who though a very excellent person, was a bitter dissenter', was horrified when, on coming into the room to remove the tea things, she saw the church cat on her carpet, begging for scraps. 'What impudence!' she exclaimed. But George and his family sternly bade her mind her manners. They fed the cat up, and were soon rewarded by seeing it become 'sleek and bonny'.

Back on the south side of the bridge the Town Trail runs off up Bridge Street, where most of Llangollen's hotels stand along the narrowing roadways. There is a constant rush and roar from the Dee as it flows over old weirs and through shallow rapids in its rocky bed below the river wall, and a glimpse of its white-flecked water opposite the Hand Hotel before you come to the church of St Collen (who gave his name to the town) on the right hand side of the road. Inside is a lovely fifteenth-century carved roof, but interest here focuses on the triangular monument within black iron railings in the churchyard just to the south of the tower. One side of the monument carries an inscription to Mrs Mary Carryl, 'Patient, Industrious, Faithful, Generous, Kind', who died in 1809. The memorial, says the inscription, was 'Reared by Two Friends who will her lofs bemoan, Till with Her Ashes . . . Here shall rest, Their own'.

Those 'Two Friends' did indeed end up in the same churchyard as their faithful, hot-tempered servant Mary Carryl, 'Molly the Bruiser' as she had been nicknamed back in their home country of Ireland. The friends – devoted to each other exclusively throughout their long lives – were Lady Eleanor Butler and Miss Sarah Ponsonby, whose own inscriptions appear on the two remaining sides of the monument. Eleanor Butler died in 1829, aged 90, and Sarah Ponsonby

> did not long survive her beloved companion . . . with whom she had lived in this valley for more than half a century of uninterrupted friendship – but they shall no more return to their House, neither shall their place know them any more (Job 7:10).

The story of Lady Eleanor Butler and Sarah Ponsonby, the celebrated 'Ladies of Llangollen', is a remarkable one. They were legends in their own lifetimes, visited by every person of distinction who came to the Vale of Llangollen, famous equally for their extraordinary, passionate mutual attachment and their eccentricity of dress and habits. They scandalized and fascinated society with their mannish dress and resemblance to two respectable, elderly clergymen, their complete indifference to what the world might think of them, and their tendency (Lady Eleanor's in particular) to give short shrift to anyone they did not care for. The Duke of Wellington visited them; so did William Wordsworth, Sir Walter Scott, Lord Castlereagh, Thomas de Quincey and Robert Southey. They had arrived in Llangollen in 1778 as two young ladies in flight from their aristocratic Irish backgrounds, filled with a romantic longing to live a simple life devoted to 'friendship, celibacy and the knitting of blue stockings'. They had not taken into account the fact that their secluded valley in North Wales lay right in the path of the Holyhead–London main road. Visitors in search of scenery soon found the Ladies in their hideaway above the town, and from then on the fashionable and famous beat an ever-widening path to their door – usually bearing a placatory gift of carved old oak or embossed leather to add to the Ladies' celebrated collection.

The journal of Lady Eleanor Butler gives a highly detailed, highly opinionated account of their 50 years together at Llangollen: troubles with servants, visits by grandees, lack of ready money, and her never-failing pleasure in the many days of 'delightful and enjoyed Retirement' with her 'Beloved' Sarah. Two extracts will give the flavour of Eleanor's breathless style:

> *Sat March 29th 1788* – Celestial lovely day. Reading, drawing. Saw a White Lamb in the Clerk's hanging Field. The Parlour getting a general scouring, sweeping and cleaning. My Beloved and I went the Home Circuit. Walked round our empty garden many times. Like it infinitely better than occupied by that Drunken idle Richard. Sweetest lovely day, close, nay even sultry. Lambs bleating. Birds singing, everything that constitutes the Beauty of solitude and retirement ... Soft fine rain. Began *Les Memoires de Madame de Maintenon*. I doubt whether the Vulgarity of stile, absurd anecdotes, and impertinent reflections will permit me to read it.

> *Fri August 7th 1789* – Light airy Clouds – purple mountains – lilac and silver rocks – hum of Bees – rush of Waters. Goat. Sheep. Cattle. Melody of Haymakers. What Weather! What a country!

The house where Eleanor Butler and Sarah Ponsonby lived during that half-century of sweet retirement, Plas Newydd, stands just outside and above Llangollen to the east, in 12 acres (15 ha) of ground mostly laid out and planted by the Ladies themselves. The Town Trail reaches it by way of Church Street and the narrow, climbing Butler Hill. The Ladies were often in dire financial straits, when handouts from relations and friends dried up; so to guarantee them a roof over their heads their faithful servant Mary Carryl bought the freehold of Plas Newydd out of her own savings and left it to her friends on her death. The present gardens with their shrubberies and topiary were created after the Ladies' tenure; their garden was more informal, planted and cared for as and when they saw fit and funds and assistance were available.

Plas Newydd itself, a simple two-storey farmhouse when the Ladies took it over in 1780, startles at first sight with its over-elaboration of black and white facings, but the great tall beech trees that surround it tone down its extravagance and put it into proper scale. The decoration of Plas Newydd, begun by the Ladies with projecting oriel windows and a porch filled with fantastic oak carving, was continued with great enthusiasm by subsequent owners, notably General John Yorke who tacked on, inside and out, carvings and ornaments that threatened to smother the little house.

It is hard to distinguish the ornamentation added to Plas Newydd by Eleanor Butler and Sarah Ponsonby from that put in by later residents. The black and white battens to the front were added by General Yorke, but the rich mass of carving all over

In the calm beauty of Plas Newydd (ABOVE), *the celebrated Ladies of Llangollen, Lady Eleanor Butler and Miss Sarah Ponsonby, lived contentedly together in the years around 1800. They received a constant stream of visitors in Plas Newydd's quirkily fantastical interior, where every surface is covered with decoration and carved ornament* (RIGHT).

the porch and front door was the idea of the Ladies. And inside only a piece-by-piece guide book description could sort out the individual parts of the fantastic jigsaw of high-relief carving and tooled leather that covers all walls, doors, nooks and crannies. The overall effect, as candlelight and firelight flickered over faces, forms and foliage, gods, kings, coats of arms, beasts and birds, must have been to make the rooms writhe into life. It's a dark, cosy house, eccentric, tasteless perhaps, yet emanating a womb-like security. The Ladies slept together in a four-poster bed, in which the excruciating pain of the migraines Eleanor suffered often had to be soothed away by her Beloved.

The Ladies strongly objected to having their portraits painted; but one of their visitors, Mary Parker, managed to sketch a likeness of them by holding her pad and pencil below the table and adding a few strokes at a time when her hostesses were not looking. The picture shows a pair of jowly old persons across the table, rather hangdog of expression, their hair cut and brushed in manly coiffures, wearing men's dark coats. In spite of their dislike of portraiture (and perhaps because of it), there was a small industry in turning out china statuettes of the Ladies, and one is on display in a bookcase in the library. Although Eleanor and Sarah would have been scandalized at the thought of the stream of visitors that now tramp through their house, their spirits may still be hovering at the dressing-room window, tartly commenting on the personal appearance of members of the public strolling through their garden.

The A539 leaves Llangollen on the north bank of the River Dee, running east under the long, bare limestone crags of Creigiau Eglwyseg. Five miles (8 km) down the valley you look across the river to see the same kind of craggy outcrop hanging above the village of Froncysyllte. These limestone faces on opposite sides of the Dee were once part of the same formation, before the landslip tore them apart and carried the rocks of Froncysyllte along to their present position. Here the canal takes a sudden southward turn to cross high above the river by means of one of the wonders of the Industrial Revolution. The Pont-Cysyllte aqueduct was built by Thomas Telford in an act of tremendous daring and ingenuity, a masterly throw of the dice of technology that achieved with simplicity what most people of the day thought was impossible.

The Ellesmere Canal was planned in the 1790s as a grand trunk route connecting the River Dee at Chester with the Severn at Shrewsbury, to bring coal and minerals from the North Wales hills to the foundries and factories of the Midlands. From the outset it proved difficult to drive the works through the hilly Border country, and when money and enthusiasm ran out the project began to fall apart. Only a useless central section was eventually finished and opened, but the building of the Pont-Cysyllte aqueduct would have justified the whole venture in terms of engineering genius.

Turn right from the A539 in the village of Trefor, along the B-road signed 'Aqueduct', to reach the Telford Inn and canal basin at the northern end of the aqueduct. The narrow-boats of Anglo-Welsh Cruisers pack the basin all the year round, waiting their turn to enter the 1007-foot-(307-m-)long iron trough full of water that runs far above the tree tops from one side of the valley to the other. Eighteen great masonry piers carry the trough across the river, towering 120 feet (37 m) from the valley bottom. There is a walkway along the aqueduct, giving a vertiginous view from the middle down to the Dee dashing in white water over shallows and an old weir. Telford and his men took ten years to build the aqueduct, which was finally opened in 1805. What drove him to take the gamble of the untried technology (the use of such a great length of cast iron had never been attempted) was the thought of the only possible alternative – a gigantic flight of locks to take the canal barges down to the Dee and up again, with all the expense and delay that would have involved. There must have been railings along both sides of the trough at one time, but those on the east side have disappeared. That edge of the aqueduct simply drops into space a hand's-breath from the barges crossing the valley. Rather them than me.

Walking south across the aqueduct you have a peaceful green view ahead, but there is a different prospect on the return journey – the gigantic steaming chimneys of a great green and silver chemical works on a hillside. Up to this point our wanderings along the Welsh Borders have been almost exclusively in beautiful agricultural and moorland country. But here we enter the industrial landscape of North Wales, ignored or lightly skipped over by most writers on this part of the world. Certainly there are scenes ahead that feature on no picture postcards – heaps of spoil, old mine-shafts and buildings, quarries and chemical plants. Nor are some of the plain, brick-built villages exactly the material of tourist brochures. Yet they are as integral a part of the Borders as any wooded valley of Monmouthshire, Black Mountain ridge or Shropshire half-timbered village in all their beauty. Chock-full of lead, coal, iron and limestone and brick clay, these northern hills have a fascination – often a bleak and stark one – all of their own. To judge them inferior landscape, unworthy of exploration, is to miss the whole flavour of this uppermost end of the journey.

Ruabon makes bricks, hard red ones. They feature in the streets of Llangollen, and their influence grows as you run east from Pont-Cysyllte into flatter country. Old terraces, new semi-detached houses, abandoned coal washeries, pubs and shops all glow bright red. The little town of Ruabon itself is full of its own products; but Park Street shows a different and older character. This short double row of squat stone houses runs from the big Wynnstay Arms Hotel to the arched gateway of Wynnstay Park, a little private village at the gate of the big house. Now a college, Wynnstay was once the home of the Williams-Wynn family, who owned more land in North Wales than anyone else. Their tiny stone hamlet in Park Street makes a strange contrast to the rest of Ruabon, which grew around the prosaic industries of quarrying, coal-mining and brick-making. It's a friendly place, where a chance remark to a stranger usually ends up in a long discussion of the town's history. Accents have a strong dash of Merseyside mixed in with the Welsh – speech tends to exit through the nose, and the letter 'r' is rolled in Liverpudlian style. You can get a fine view over the red ranks of Ruabon from Gardden Lodge, a discreet little collection of houses strung out around the Iron Age fort of Pen-y-gardden north of the town.

The brick and tile works lies 2 miles (3 km) north of Ruabon, in the valley to the east of the ridge-top village of Johnstown. Here are enormous mounds of red and black spoil, long runs of conveyor belt, hoists, yellow tipper trucks and low works buildings. Black dust and sludge spread all over the place between the hillocks of misshapen and discarded bricks. The bricks have good, practical names – Red Pavers and Black Pavers. Bricks and quarry tiles that have passed muster stand in polythene packs by the hundred thousand in the brickworks yard. In this place the marriage between successful industry and landscape devastation is seen at its most striking. But just to the east along the B5426 the countryside resumes green tranquillity as it rolls through open parkland and flat river valley grazing fields to come to Bangor-is-y-coed on the banks of the River Dee.

The countryside around Llangollen is not for those who might suffer from vertigo. The breathtaking natural view from the pathway along Offa's Dyke at Creigiau Eglwyseg (ABOVE) is matched by the hair-raising man-made walk across the Pont-Cysyllte aqueduct which Thomas Telford built high above the River Dee (LEFT).

A sixteenth-century bridge leads across the river into the village – a bridge built of large chunks of red and yellow sandstone, giving a nice patchwork effect, enhanced by the blurring and softening of the stone through centuries of weathering. The bridge is too narrow for modern traffic, and there is a more modern structure just up the road that brings you through characterless bungalow housing estates into the short main street which runs down to the old bridge. This is the old, quiet heart of the village, where the handsome red sandstone church stands above the river near the site of the first monastery to be established in Britain. The monks of Bangor-is-y-coed settled here as early as AD 180. Their story ended in tragedy, and in the birth of a nation. In 607 the

The arms of the Williams-Wynn family, who once dominated this entire region, adorn the public house at Johnstown named after their former family home.

Northumbrian King Ethelfrid descended to crush the Christian Britons of North Wales, and killed 1200 monks of Bangor after they had refused his command to pray for a Northumbrian victory. Until the battle the North Welsh had been part of a Celtic grouping of peoples that included those inhabiting Cumbria and the lowlands of Scotland, but after Ethelfrid's victory they found themselves forced back into the lands west of Chester and rallied round a new name, the 'Cymry' or Comrades – the first stirrings of a purely Welsh nationalism. The present-day vicar of Bangor-is-y-coed, Philip Owens is also a poet: you can buy a book of his fine poems in the church.

The shallow, rolling landscape continues eastward across the border and into Cheshire as the B5069 takes you on towards Malpas. The hedges along the road here are cut in the traditional way, an A-shape whose broad base gives shelter for the small birds and animals that have been driven out of less fortunate farmland where hedges are slashed thin or ripped out completely. This sense of careful management extends to the

Glimpsed through the arches of the
sixteenth-century bridge at Bangor-
is-y-Coed (ABOVE), the parish church
stands near the site of the earliest
monastery in Britain, in a region
where the very first stirrings of
Welsh nationalism were to be felt
in the Dark Ages. Malpas, now just
across into Cheshire, perilously
straddled the border in the early
Middle Ages. Its quiet, open market
place, with the elegant steps
leading up to St Oswald's church
(LEFT) give no sense of Malpas's
troubled past.

In the substantial parish church at Malpas, which was largely rebuilt around 1500 (ABOVE), *flamboyantly carved wooden screens divide the north and south chapels from the main body. In them, elaborate tombs to the Cholmondeley and Brereton families are placed, of which the early Stuart alabaster effigies of Sir Hugh and Lady Mary Cholmondeley* (LEFT) *are the most exquisitely and tenderly carved.*

little town of Malpas, 4 miles (6½ km) into England. Malpas derives its names from the Norman description of the 'bad pass' through the boggy marshes of the Shropshire–Cheshire plain, but there's nothing bad now about this well-founded place, based round an open market place from which run streets sloping up and down. Every view looks good from the centre of Malpas, cradled between Georgian and older buildings. But as a Border town, Malpas has had its moments of terror in times past. During the twelfth and thirteenth centuries, when conflict between England and Wales was at its height, the parish of Malpas lay with a foot in either country. After battles around the town, the English dead had to be buried where they fell in the fields, since no-one dared to bring them to Malpas churchyard. Neither did local Englishmen dare to come to mass on Easter Sunday, in case the Welshmen of Malpas should attack them.

The church of St Oswald, perched on a ridge at the eastern edge of the town, is a safe place for Englishmen these days; the only attack they are likely to suffer is one of pleasure when contemplating the beautiful sandstone, weathered and faded to the most delicate pink, and the superb effigies of the Breretons and Cholmondeleys who successively ruled Malpas in Tudor times. Sir Randle and Lady Eleanor Brereton lie in the south chapel of the church, Sir Hugh and Lady Mary Cholmondeley in the north chapel. These are wonderful examples of the carver's skill. How long must the artists have laboured to shape the details of Sir Randle Brereton's armour and his wife's embroidery, or the Elizabethan ruffs in multiple folds round the necks of the Cholmondeleys? The Brereton couple lie long-faced and pious, with noble noses held aloft; the faces of Hugh and Mary Cholmondeley, by contrast, are quietly smiling and touched with humour. I would rather have dinner with the Cholmondeleys than with those stiff and solemn Breretons.

If Malpas suffered because of its border position, so did the twin villages of Farndon and Holt that face each other across their bridge over the River Dee some 8 miles (13 km) to the north-west. The national boundary runs down the middle of the river here, and there has always been rivalry between Farndon (English) and Holt (Welsh). The narrow fourteenth-century sandstone bridge is called Holt Bridge by those on the west bank of the river, Farndon Bridge by those on the east.

In medieval times there was a gatehouse on the Holt or Welsh end of the bridge to emphasize the division; and during the Civil War it was the scene of one of those skirmishes that had little or no effect on the general course of the conflict but which lodged immovably in local mythology. On 9 November 1643, Sir William Brereton and Colonel Thomas Mytton brought a force of 2000 Parliamentarian soldiers to the bridge, intending to cross it and capture Royalist Holt. The inhabitants of Holt, forewarned of the impending attack, lit beacons and 'rang the church bells backwards' to call everyone on the Welsh side to arms. The Roundheads, pretending to launch a crossing of the river downstream of the bridge, managed to lure enough men of Holt away from their posts to get across the bridge and destroy the drawbridge of the gatehouse; but further than that they could not go. Holt and the western end of the bridge remained in Royalist hands for another two years, until the tide had turned decisively in favour of Parliament. But Cheshire had its Royalist gentlemen too: four of them feature together with their followers – pikemen and halberdiers – in a stained-glass window in the south aisle of the church at Farndon.

You can stretch your legs hereabouts on a fine walk upriver beside the Dee from Holt, past the crumbling stump of Holt Castle (built in the late thirteenth century) and on along the meanders of the river. Then strike westwards on the B5102 to cross the A541 north of Wrexham. Here are the eastern outskirts of a mineral working district whose isolated chapels and tiny industrial settlements with uncompromising biblical names – Horeb, Mount Sion, Sodom, Babylon, Babell – are scattered in deep valleys and across steep hillsides and scarred upland moors. Brymbo, 4 miles (6½ km) north-west of Wrexham, sits on top of huge deposits of coal and iron ore; and in the nineteenth century iron, and later steel, came pouring out of the enormous works here. Steel is still made in the huge flat sheds, clean and featureless seen from below, but heaped up behind with a great black morass of sludge and spoil.

Beyond Brymbo you drive north and west by narrow lanes into high hill country where the lonely farms stand side by side with green spoil heaps of the now defunct coal- and lead-mining industries. On the far side of the B5102 rises Hope Mountain, a long ridge where little hamlets such as Cymau and Ffrith are tucked away in side valleys under wooded slopes. The lanes are bent into hairpins, rising up and over the hills with tremendous views over a remote landscape seldom visited by tourists. The chapel at Horeb is a perfect example of the simple, box-like buildings put up for the Dissenter miners of the nineteenth century who followed a large number of only slightly differentiated sects. Up a stony side lane with a single wind-blown farm for company, the chapel stands plain, stark and defiant, a symbol of religion with no frills whatsoever, in a countryside with the same characteristics.

This is the landscape captured by Daniel Owen (1836–95), the tailor of Mold, in his novels written in the second half of the nineteenth century. Owen has no fame in the English-speaking literary world, since all his novels were written in Welsh. 'Not for the wise and learned have I written, but for the common people', runs the inscription under his verdigrised statue outside the library in Mold. Owen's works were well known by ordinary Welsh men and women (those who could read), but unpopular with Methodist leaders in the area who felt that they gave an unhealthily 'untruthful' view of life. Perhaps they objected to the honesty of passages like this one from *Gwen Tomos*:

> If there are lead mines or coal-pits in the vicinity, one will usually find two, three or even four small chapels. In some places two chapels exist within a stone's throw of one another, eyeing each other jealously. It is a frequent sight to see two neighbours who agree on all matters except religion, passing each other of Sundays to attend a chapel a considerable distance away, having rejected one nearer, because the one had too much water and the other too little.

Owen's subjects – ordinary life in ordinary places, the stirrings of unrest in lead-mines and coal-pit communities in the hills around Mold, the first flickerings of Trade Unionism and strife with the owners and bosses – were also hard for the targets of his criticism to accept. None of the English translations of his books is now in print, unfortunately, though you can buy them in Welsh in the bookshops of Mold. The library has a couple of the translated versions, and a little display corner devoted to Owen, featuring his broad-brimmed hat, his stick and spectacles, and a reproduction of a nineteenth-century tailor's shop.

An angel, up on the nave arcade of Mold parish church, holds a shield which bears the fleur-de-lys of the King of France, a title which the tudor monarchs still claimed. Tudor roses adorn the timber roof above.

Mold's main street slopes gently uphill, wide and handsome. Half-way up is the fifteenth-century church of St Mary, with fine Tudor masonry elaborately carved above the nave arcades, and a splendid dark wooden roof over the north aisle of close-clustered panels carved with Tudor roses. At the top of the street a pathway winds round and up the motte of Bailey Hill, whose Norman castle has long since vanished. The River Alyn ran red with English blood on the day in 1199 when Llewelyn the Great captured the castle. These days it's a quiet, grassy grandstand surrounded by tall beech trees, from which there is a fine view down over old Mold; you can also see new Mold in the shape of Clwyd County Council's buildings standing like giant egg-boxes by the road to Flint.

On the way to Flint, turn off at Northop along the minor road towards Rhosesmor, stopping after 1 mile ($1\frac{1}{2}$ km) where a long wood slopes down to meet the lane. A raised bank about 5 feet ($1\frac{1}{2}$ m) high comes up from the south, studded with oak trees, to cross the lane and run north as a rampart just inside the edge of the wood. This is one of the best preserved sections of Wat's Dyke, an earthwork that runs from Oswestry northwards to the coast, which was built shortly after AD 700, more than half a century before the far greater and more celebrated Offa's Dyke. Wat's Dyke defined the western line of the kingdom of Mercia at that time, an exercise in line-holding until the mighty Offa came along to settle and fix the boundary permanently. Nowadays it is all but forgotten. There are no guides to Wat's Dyke, and no long-distance walkers step it out. Rabbits, badgers and foxes have the best use of it, burrowing into the soft soil thrown up almost 1300 years ago.

At Flint you complete your south-to-north journey along the Welsh Borders, and (if you don't mind a boot full of mud) can dip your foot in the estuary of the River Dee to celebrate the achievement. It has to be said that Flint is not a lovely town by any stretch of the imagination. There has been an explosion of insensitive development − baldly towering blocks of flats, badly designed shops, bleak housing estates − right in the heart of the town. In fact, bleakness is the first word that comes to mind when thinking of Flint. In rain or winter mists off the estuary it can look as cold, hard and grey as its namesake in stone. But the castle remains, on a green mound of rock overlooking the wide estuary, are commanding and impressive even in their ruinous state. Flint was the first of the castles built by Edward I, put up in 1277 to guard the shipping up and down the Dee before he had properly subdued the Welsh. On the right of the moat bridge stands the huge round donjon, a defensive structure unique among British fortresses which was detached from the main body of the castle and connected to it by a drawbridge. It was intended as a last place of retreat for hard-pressed defenders of the castle, who could isolate themselves inside its walls of red and yellow sandstone, 10 feet (3 m) thick, and hope for better days. Flint Castle was the scene of the surrender of Richard II (1377–99) to his adversary Henry Bolingbroke in August 1399. Even Richard's greyhound, so the story goes, deserted his master in his hour of need and sidled off to lick the hand of Bolingbroke. Shakespeare depicted the moment of confrontation between the defeated king and his triumphant enemy in Act III of *Richard II*, in the scene entitled 'Before Flint Castle':

> *Boling.*: My gracious Lord, I come but for mine own,
> *K. Rich.*: Your own is yours, and I am yours, and all.

Through the broken masonry of the donjon's upper windows you look eastward up the estuary, over the bare saltings and mud flats where curlews bubble and waders pick over the tideline, to the distant sheds, pylons and chimneys of the gigantic Shotton Steelworks complex on the marshlands where Wales meets the Wirral peninsula.

From Flint, strike west by minor roads to climb into the barren moorland of Halkyn Mountain, a ridge rising to almost 1000 feet (300 m) whose heart is veined with lead seams that kept miners in work for 2000 years, from Roman times right up until a few years ago. Medieval workers mined Halkyn lead for roof coverings. Seventeenth- and eighteenth-century landowners opened up new mines on their own patches, and turned their lead into gold for their purses. Cornish miners flocked to the area to find work and put their expertise to good use. The London Lead Company installed steam pumping engines in the eighteenth century and mined lead until flooding forced them to give up.

Even when the lodes began to give out in the early years of this century the small-scale operators went on, until the last of the Halkyn mines closed in 1958. But mining still starts up sporadically here and there.

The upper ranges of Halkyn Mountain are bleak in the extreme, but it is not the bleakness of poor subdued Flint on its muddy shore. Up here it is all rock-studded moorland of gorse, bracken and heather, bitten and delved into quarry cliffs and bowls, lumpy with old spoil heaps of forgotten lead-mines, dotted with widely strung mining settlements. Pwll-clai (O.S. ref. 187738) is a good example: a few cottages whose tiny windows and steeply sloping roofs bear witness to the wildness of the mountain's weather, a handful of rickety old sheds, all scattered over a bumpy green area on each side of the road. As an antidote to this harsh landscape, dive into the Glan-yr-afon Inn (196738) on the crossroads below the settlement of Dolphin. The Glan-yr-afon is a bright and cheerful pub, serving excellent meals and good beer, whose landlord is an enthusiast over local history. His home-made display inside the pub tells the story of the lead-mines of Halkyn in great detail. One aspect both fascinates and fills the claustrophobic reader with dread – the account of the great Sea Level Tunnel begun in 1897 and driven into the mountain from Bagillt on the Dee estuary to drain the lead workings. Eventually the tunnel extended 10 miles (16 km) inland, revealing twelve unsuspected lodes of lead on its way. The landlord told me that from the bottom of a shaft just below the pub one can see the light at the seaward end of the Sea Level Tunnel, a pinprick of light 3 miles (5 km) away. Didn't I long to see that sight? I did not.

The small town of Holywell lies at the northern end of Halkyn Mountain, a tangle of tight little streets that leads down the hill to another of the Seven Wonders of Wales, the holy well of St Winefride. The well is still a place of pilgrimage, where sick and sad people come in hopes of finding a cure in the dark, bubbling waters of the little well in its ornate crypt beneath a chapel perched against the valley side. There is a souvenir shop below the chapel, but once inside the dark crypt complete silence takes hold. Votive candles flicker, casting a faint glow up to the carved and embossed fan vaulting of the ceiling. On one side hang old photographs of forests of cripples' crutches stacked against the wall by their owners after miraculous cures had set them leaping and praising God around the well. The focus of all these acts of faith is a little bowl of quietly seething water under the central canopy in the crypt. Steps lead down into a side bath. The water is beautifully cold, pumped into the well these days from a reservoir – mining operations on Halkyn Mountain interfered with the flow of the spring in 1917, causing it to dry up.

The spring had its beginnings in a manner not uncommon in Celtic mythology – the falling to earth of the severed head of a martyred saint. St Justinian on Ramsey Island off the Pembrokeshire coast had the same effect. Here at Holywell the saintly victim was a local princess, Winefride, niece of the hermit St Beuno who built a chapel on the site in the early seventh century. When Prince Caradoc tried to seduce her, Winefride ran for sanctuary towards her uncle's chapel, but she never reached it. Caradoc caught up with her, and in a fury cut off her head. A spring of water burst out of the ground at the place where it fell. St Beuno, hearing the commotion, rushed out of his chapel and picked up his niece's head. He washed it in the spring, fitted it back on to her shoulders – and she lived on, to become an abbess and die in her own good time in AD 650. The would-be rapist Caradoc was not so lucky, however. As soon as he had done the dreadful deed, the ground opened up and swallowed him.

St Winefride's well soon became a place of pilgrimage. In 1490 Margaret Beaufort, the mother of King Henry VII, gave most of the money that built the chapel and crypt over the well; there is a carving of her head in the ceiling. Sufferers came to pray and immerse themselves in the little bath beside the well. The red moss that grew on the well's stony floor was said to be coloured by the blood of St Winefride. Pilgrimage ceased after the Reformation – such acts were punishable by death, but perhaps the call of martyrdom had lost some of its attraction. In the eighteenth century it resumed, however, and is still going strong. Dr Johnson came to view the holy well during his tour of Wales in 1774, and was upset by the sight of a naked woman taking a curative dip. In these cooler-blooded days the suggestion on the notices is for visitors to dip only their hands in the water.

Another relic of ancient faith stands 3 miles (5 km) north-east of Holywell in a field by a lonely crossroads (129787). The exact purpose in the minds of those who raised Maen Achwyfan, the Stone of Lamentation, is unguessable, but they created a beautiful and strange work of art on this isolated saddle of ground. Maen Achwyfan is a superb Celtic cross, nearly 11 feet (3 m) high – the tallest in Britain – and erected in about AD 1000. The top of the column is rounded and carved with a wheel cross; the massive shaft is covered with interlaced carving from top to bottom. There are three bands of carving – rounded swirls, a sunburst emblem, and crudely squared, interwoven lattice-work. Though there is a Viking touch to the patterns, the whole effect of Maen Achwyfan is Celtic – wild and forceful, a wonderful creation.

From the crossroads a narrow lane takes you down out of the Celtic mists and slap into the modern world at Mostyn on the shores of the estuary. Mostyn Docks advertise themselves as 'The Best Small Port In The North West', and they are certainly busy with the timber, steel and waste paper that pile high on the dockside. At low tide the big freighters lie alongside, stranded in mud, their holds dipped into by tall cranes on rails. Coal boats and passenger vessels once left Mostyn for Ireland, and the old stone slipways and quays that served the Irish trade still stand beyond the modern goods sheds. After signing an indemnity form in the Mostyn Docks company's offices, you can wander among these busy quays, and out along the great tongue of grassed-over iron slag which the now-defunct Mostyn Iron and Steel Company's works disgorged into the estuary. This black-sided, hump-backed pier of slag sticks out half a mile (1 km) into the water among flat grey banks of slimy mud. From the tip there is a wonderful view over the estuary to the coastline of the Wirral, and back along the Welsh shore, from Shotton Steelworks down in the east round to the marshy Point of Ayr to the west.

Just inland of the docks, Mostyn Hall stands serenely in a wooded park. The Mostyn family were related to the Tudors, and the Hall features in a royal escape story worthy of that other great princely fugitive, Charles II. Henry Tudor, then Earl of Richmond but soon to be crowned King Henry VII, was hiding at Mostyn Hall with his uncle Jasper, Earl of Pembroke, in the tense months of 1485 leading up to the Battle of Bosworth. Henry Tudor was about to eat dinner with his Mostyn host when a force of men loyal to King Richard III arrived to secure him. As they clattered towards the dining chamber, Henry leaped out of his seat and through the window. Before the host could move, the king's men had burst into the room, their leader demanding to know why there was an extra place at table. Mostyn thought on his feet. An old family custom, he answered coolly; laying a spare place in case an unexpected guest should turn up.

*Almost a thousand years old, and standing some 11 feet high, the Celtic cross of
Maen Achwyfan is one of the proudest of all emblems of the tenacity of the Christian
faith that flourished in the Welsh borders.*

Talking of which – would the officer like to fulfil the tradition and sit down to dine in that place? The offer was accepted, and the fugitive outside the window had time to get clear.

Now comes the homeward run, south from the shores of the Dee's broad estuary to the steep valley of the same river back at Llangollen, by way of the beautiful Vale of Clwyd. The valley runs for 20 miles (32 km) south and east, narrowing all the way, a green sweep of prosperous, peaceful farming country, one of the most fertile valleys in the Welsh Borders. The Vale of Clwyd is founded on sandstone, which accounts for its warm richness and makes a clear contrast with the hard Silurian slates and shales of the Clwydian Hills that accompany it on the east all the way along. Down in the valley all is rich and soft; up on the hills all is bare and wild. These Clwydian Hills are the highest ground between Snowdonia and the Derbyshire Peak District – not very high as hills go, but an impressive barrier between the industrial mining area on their eastern flanks and the rural valley west of them. At their highest point, Moel Famau, they reach only 1820 feet (555 m), but the dips between the heights are shallow, and the impression is of a continuous, undulating ridge. Walkers on the Offa's Dyke path have a clear run along the crest of the ridge, and earlier travellers, too, appreciated the height and all-round views afforded by the Clwydian Hills. Bronze Age traders established a track up here along which they carried goods to the shores of the Dee estuary and the boats across to Ireland; and Iron Age people built a string of six forts on the moels or rounded hilltops of the range. The Clwydian Hills are magnificent walking country, and equally satisfying for less energetic car-borne visitors. Our route down the Vale of Clwyd keeps mostly to the A525 road (reached via the lanes south-west from Mostyn and then the A55), for the sake of the views that it gives up to the ridges and crests of the hills.

The chief town of the Vale of Clwyd is Denbigh, set on the western slope of the valley looking across to the Clwydian Hills. Denbigh is all slopes and hills, in fact, rising and falling this way and that in a maze of short streets and long lanes. The centre of the town, reached up a long and steep hill, has escaped improvement; there is no shortage in High Street or in Crown Square of cruel orange brickwork, terracotta and ambitious neo-classical designs, but not a single building intrudes or jars. It's a lived-in and well-settled town, where you are likely to see a lorry piled high with bales of straw lurching its way past the market stalls in High Street, or farmers from the hills arguing companionably over the doors of their mud-splattered Land Rovers. There's a strong sense of the country come to town in Denbigh, reinforced by the grand view east from Crown Square of the enormous domed heads of Moel Arthur and Moel Llys-y-coed filling the horizon. There are back rows (such as Back Row) winding behind the main streets, narrow lanes packed with old half-timbered pubs, courtyards and bookshops selling children's books in Welsh – *Superted yng Nghastell Iasoer* ('Superted in the Ice-cold Castle'), or *Rympelstiltsgin* ('Rumpelstiltskin').

Down at the bottom of the town, just off the A525 road north, the shell of a church built in about 1300 stands modestly down a side track, unsignposted and largely unvisited, three stone walls with a fine three-tier east window whose tracery was long ago

The marshy promontory of the Point of Ayr, with its lighthouse to guide vessels, stands away to the seaward side of the bustling Mostyn Docks on the Dee estuary, the northernmost point on the Border itineraries.

The ruined Carmelite friary at Denbigh (ABOVE) was founded by the brave Sir John Salusbury, who allegedly slew a dragon that lived below Denbigh Castle (RIGHT). The castle withstood many onslaughts through the fourteenth and fifteenth centuries, but it finally fell victim, as did many of the Border castles, to the onslaught of Parliament's forces in the mid seventeenth-century Civil Wars.

bricked in. The church belonged to a Carmelite Friary established in 1285 by Sir John Salusbury, a red-blooded man with an eventful life story. He had two thumbs on each hand, which may have given him the strength he displayed when felling a lion at the Tower of London with one blow of his fist. Sir John joined the Crusades, and also fought and defeated a dragon who lived in a cave below Denbigh Castle. When the bold knight raised the monster's severed head to the people crowding the town walls, they are said to have shouted with one voice: *Dim Bych*! – 'No more dragon!' – thereby giving the town its name.

From the west end of High Street runs Highgate. Half-way along, a steep flight of steps on the left, paved with slates jammed in on end, climbs sharply up past little terraces and courtyards perched on the hillside, with glimpses over slate roofs and tiny green patches of garden. At the top you emerge under the massive arch of the Burgess Tower, built of great slabs of greenish-yellow sandstone, straddling the road up to Denbigh Castle. Continue climbing past the solitary tower of St Hilary's church (built in 1334 as the castle chapel), looking down to your left on to the ruined arches of 'Leicester's Folly'. These are all that remains of a great church planned by Robert Dudley (1532/3–88), Earl of Leicester and favourite of Elizabeth I, after she had given him Denbigh Castle. He began the church in 1579, but never got very far with it.

Up on the very crest of the hill stands the big gatehouse of Denbigh Castle, ruinous and jagged, its walls punched full of holes, but still a powerful and dominant piece of architecture. Henry de Lacy was placed in Denbigh by Edward I as soon as his conquest of the Welsh was complete in 1282; given the lordship of Denbigh, De Lacy went straight ahead with building a strongly fortified castle. He had not quite finished the work when the Welsh captured the castle in 1294. On retaking Denbigh, the English overlords strengthened and restrengthened their stronghold, extending the outer walls to embrace the whole town. (You can walk a partial circuit of these old walls after collecting the key to the gate from the castle curator.)

Denbigh Castle was fated to have a turbulent history. After the brief Welsh reoccupation of 1294 there was a century of comparative stability before, in 1399, Harry Hotspur requisitioned it as his base of operations in North Wales. In 1402 Owain Glyndŵr burned the town, in spite of the supposed security of its position within the castle walls, and in 1468 Jasper Tudor repeated the exercise. After that, the townspeople began to build outside the walls. Twice bitten . . .! During the Civil War Charles I stayed here briefly, in flight from defeat at the Battle of Rowton Moor near Chester. Then the Roundheads captured the castle after an epic siege of 11 months, and put paid to its three and a half centuries of stout defence by slighting it.

Sheep nibble the grass of the inner ward, whose walls were so effectively pulled to pieces during the slighting and in the ensuing centuries that there are views all round the circle between the broken stubs of masonry. The best view is from high up in the eastern tower, over the town roofs and out across the Vale of Clwyd to the majestic, swelling wall of the Clwydian Hills.

The highest point of the hills at 1820 feet (554 m), Moel Famau, is seen from the walls of Denbigh Castle as a domed head wearing a tiny pillbox hat. To discover the true identity of that flat little excrescence on the noblest peak of the Clwydian Hills, cross the valley from Denbigh and drive south for 6 miles (10 km) on the B5429 to Llandbedr-Dyffryn-Clwyd, turning left here on to a narrow mountain road that snakes up and over

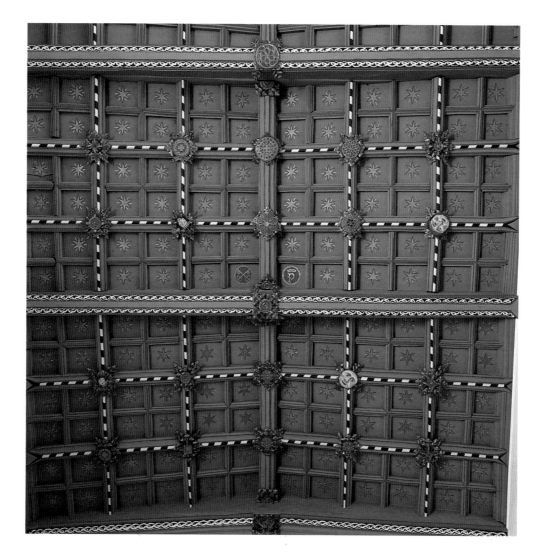

The oak ceiling in St Peter's church, Ruthin, is a superb example of the craftmanship of early Tudor woodworking, divided into hundreds of panels bearing Tudor roses and a maze of coloured faces and patterns.

Bwlch Penbarra, the pass under Moel Famau. As you climb, look back and round you to enjoy the contrast between the lush green valley behind and the hard moorland each side. There are two car parks on Bwlch Penbarra, one just over the crest where the trees come down to the road, and the other half-way down through the plantation.

Leave the car at this second car park and climb up a steep, stony track waymarked with blue (easy) and red (steep). The red route, though steep enough, is no mountaineer's struggle. It climbs steadily between the conifers, straight up the south-eastern flank of Moel Famau on a carpet of pine needles for 1000 feet (300 m), leaving the trees behind for a final short and knee-cracking scramble up a stony slide to a stile on the crown of the hill. Here the pillbox hat is revealed as a broad stump of masonry sitting across the top of Moel Famau. This is all that remains of the great Jubilee Tower, erected in 1820 to mark the sixtieth year of the reign of George III, and blown down in a gale in

1862. Steps lead up to a platform on top, where direction plaques tell you what you can see in the enormous panorama all round, one of the biggest and best views in all the Borders. Honesty compels me to admit that the furthest view I had when I climbed Moel Famau was of sodden sheep a stone's throw away; a cloud had settled itself infuriatingly over the hilltop. But the information boards told me what I should be seeing – Snowdon and Cader Idris, 35 and 40 miles (56 and 64 km) respectively, away in the west; Rhyl, 20 miles (32 km), and Crosby, 28 miles (45 km), in the north, on each side of the great sweep of Liverpool Bay; to the south the rest of the Clwydian range; and in the east the Dee estuary narrowing to Runcorn Bridge, 25 miles (40 km) off. All the curses I could muster, however, failed to shift that clinging mist, leaving me with Clwydian sheep as a poor consolation.

If you, too, find these scenic glories hidden in the mist, there is compensation down in the valley in the little, lively town of Ruthin 8 miles (13 km) south of Denbigh on the A525. Ruthin has a splendid Craft Centre on its northern edge, grouped round a courtyard where you can see workers busy at glass-blowing, pottery, embroidery, jewellery-making, sculpting, bronze-casting, engraving, print-making, pewterwork, candle-making and stone-carving. You can buy samples of their work straight from the chisel and palette, before plunging in among the busy streets of Ruthin.

The heart of the town is St Peter's Square, lined on all sides with splendid old buildings: the Myddleton Arms with its many small dormer windows in tiers on a red-tiled roof; the handsome square Castle Hotel next door; the National Westminster Bank, a half-timbered building dating from 1401 which still has the stump of a gallows-beam projecting from its eaves to show its past function as the Court House of Ruthin (judge, condemn and hang in one convenient place); and the brown and white half-timbering of Exmewe Hall, built in about 1500 and now housing Barclays Bank. On the pavement stands Maen Huail, a waist-high lump of limestone on which legend says that King Arthur severed the head of his rival in love, the unlucky Huail. The sole blot on this delectable townscape is – of course – the ugly clock tower, which no self-respecting Border town could be without in Victorian days.

Just off the south side of St Peter's Square stands the collegiate church of St Peter, behind fine wrought-iron gates. The great treasure of St Peter's is the Tudor oak roof over the north aisle, given to the church by Henry VII (1485–1509) soon after he came to the throne as a gesture of gratitude to all the local gentry who had helped him on his way to victory and the crown at Bosworth Field. The dark oak roof, its bosses picked out in bright paint during the 1960s, is divided into more than 400 little square panels, each of which is carved with a different motif. The bosses carry Tudor roses, geometric patterns, foliage and a number of leering and grinning faces which the restorer repainted in a vigorous, cartoon-like style, cleverly using shading to make cheeks bulge and eyes pop.

On the north wall is a little brass to Edward Goodman, mercer of Ruthin, and his wife Cicelye – he died in 1560 aged 84, she in 1583 aged 90 – and their five daughters and three sons. The second of these, Gabriel Goodman, rose to become Dean of Westminster, a powerful prelate who never forgot his home town. His various endowments made Ruthin the educational centre of North Wales. To the north of the church stands the Grammar School which he founded in 1574, built of creamy stone; and to the east are the diminutive Christ's Hospital almshouses which were his gift to the town in 1590, grouped round a little courtyard.

St Peter's church was founded in the early fourteenth century as a collegiate church, and the cloisters where the small community of priests lived still stand, a solid two-storey building of big red sandstone and white limestone blocks attached to the north wall of the church. The vicar of Ruthin has been called by the title 'Warden' ever since the foundation of the church, and the Wardens lived in the cloisters up until 1954, with their organist right under their eye in his own brick-built extension. Now, by a twist of history, the cloisters house the rooms of the Gabriel Goodman Masonic Lodge.

Clwyd Street runs north-east from St Peter's Square, down the hill to where the old town jail now houses the records department of the county. Opposite this grim fortress, its tiny windows still barred, Mill Street winds up to a footway running round the crenellated walls of Ruthin Castle. It was Lord de Grey of Ruthin who sparked the main phase of Owain Glyndŵr's rebellion in 1400 when he seized some of the Glyndŵr lands. That was the signal for the Welsh to rise under their charismatic leader and launch an attack on Ruthin Castle. They did not succeed in capturing the castle, but made an excellent job of burning the town, leaving only one house standing. The castle met its end at the hands of the Roundheads, who slighted it in 1647 after capturing it. Nowadays it forms part of a very grand hotel, its remains scenically draped in ivy.

There are many other old and historic buildings in Ruthin – a stroll along the triangle of Castle Street, Record Street and Well Street shows off a good sample of them. Before you leave St Peter's Square, spare time for a short side-step down Market Street to find two massive civic buildings facing each other – the huge Town Hall and market in light grey and the bulky County Offices in dark red, a titanic clash of limestone and sandstone.

From Ruthin the A525 runs on down the Vale of Clwyd, to climb across the southern end of the Clwydian Hills by the snaking Nant-y-Garth pass, where trees crowd the steep, rocky hillsides high over the road. The pastoral beauty of Clwyd is left behind and below as you re-enter mineral hill country and cross an open moor to reach Bwlchgwyn. There is an excellent geological museum here, beside the Milestone Inn, its grounds dotted with remnants of the area's industrial past – the winding wheels of a pit's headgear, the brick dome of a beehive kiln where Ruabon bricks and tiles were once fired, gears and shafts, cables and engines of various sorts. In the museum you follow a trail lined with geological maps, displays of the industries of coal, cement, steel, aluminium and limestone, and thousands of dull or glinting specimens of the rocks that gave local people 2000 years of livelihood – flowstone, breccia, sphalerite, calcite, quartz – some familiar, others known only to those well versed in the remoter depths of geology. In this little museum you can see knitted together the various underlying threads of the landscape and its industries through which you have been wandering.

The last long road back to Llangollen trails through the mining settlements of Minera and New Brighton – the latter a tiny collection of stone-built terraces high on a hillside on a short road to nowhere, named with more optimism than realism by its founding inhabitants. From New Brighton a single-track road climbs under limestone crags and over the broad, desolate shoulder of Esclusham Mountain, a deserted, dark moorland where crumbling stone walls run among sedgy bogs and wide aprons of heather. Pale grey spoil heaps of lead-mining lie on the moor, adding to the lonely and barren atmosphere of the mountain. Then ahead a wonderful view opens out, down a cleft to Creigiau Eglwyseg, the bared teeth of limestone that tower above the valley north of Llangollen. The mountain road plunges and bends steeply downhill, with an eagle's eye view down on to the Tudor manor house at World's End. The name perfectly fits the spot, as remote as could be in its narrow dell below the great crags. The house has a beauty unenhanced by any modern restoration; it simply stands there under its solid, tooth-topped chimneys and stone-tiled roof, its herring-bone half-timbering faded and stained in a way that would have the inhabitants of Weobley or Ledbury reaching for the blacking brush and whitewash. A solid block of masonry forms the footing of the building, over whose south-western door hangs a sign: MDLXIII ELIZABETH REGINA. Tiny arched windows break the blank face of the west wall. Below the house is a run of barns that must be equally old. Stand in front of the house and listen. Not a single sound outside the natural ones of trickling water from the stream, wind blowing down the valley and sheep bleating on the hillsides. World's End, for sure.

Is this the spot where, in the year 1108, the beautiful Nesta lay – perhaps reluctantly, perhaps willingly – in the arms of her impetuous captor Owain ap Cadwgan, Prince of Powys, or is it a couple of miles down the valley at Plas yn Eglwyseg? This is a

Bearing its date of 1563 and the dedication to Queen Elizabeth, the house at World's End below Creigiau Eglwyseg stands perfect and untouched in the remote beauty of the Welsh borders.

romantic story worth any number of retellings. Owain, by all accounts a hot-headed and obstreperous young man, was inflamed by tales of the beauty of Nesta, 'Helen of Wales', the wife of the Norman baron Gerald of Windsor. Nesta had served a term as concubine to Henry I, and had borne him a son before being married off to Gerald of Windsor, the king's Constable in Pembrokeshire. Now the fiery young Welsh prince determined to have and hold the beauty for himself. Gathering a group of supporters, he made his way south to Gerald's castle at Cilgerran on the River Teifi in Pembrokeshire, set fire to the castle, and in the confusion grabbed Nesta and her two children. In true lover's style he galloped off with her, back to his hunting lodge in the wilds of Eglwyseg, leaving the Norman lord of Cilgerran to scramble to safety in his nightshirt by way of a rope lowered down the unsavoury chute of his own garderobe.

Henry, wild with anger at this humiliation of his friend, seized the lands of Cadwgan, Owain's father, setting off a train of fighting and burning across the countryside. Under parental pressure the young prince returned the children to their father, but for a long time he refused to release Nesta. When at last Owain let her go, he prudently fled across the water to Ireland and waited for the fuss to die down. But Gerald of Windsor neither forgave nor forgot. He bided his time, until Owain ap Cadwgan had returned to Wales with the hatchet apparently buried. At last the day came when the two rivals found themselves on the same side in battle; and then Gerald slew Owain in sweet, if long delayed, revenge.

The final stopping point in our exploration of the Welsh Borders stands guard where the Eglwyseg valley meets the Vale of Llangollen. Castell Dinas Bran, the ruined hilltop castle so conspicuous from the streets of Llangollen on its knoll, is reached by a stiff climb from a side road just north-east of the town (227432). There were various Welsh castles up here on this superb high vantage point, wooden structures succeeding one another, until in the 1230s Prince Madoc ap Gruffydd Maelor built a stone castle from shale dug out of a deep trench that lies across the southern part of the hilltop.

Castell Dinas Bran was not an auspicious place for the founding family. Gruffydd Madoc, son of Madoc ap Gruffydd Maelor, lost it to Llewelyn the Last in 1257, regained it soon after and promptly died. Madog, son of Gruffydd Madoc (shades of J.R.R. Tolkien!) lost the castle in 1276 during King Edward I's drive against Llewelyn the Last, got it back the following year – and promptly died. Then in 1282 the deaths of Llewelyn and his brother Dafydd brought the final crushing of Welsh hopes of self-governance, and Castell Dinas Bran fell into disuse. On such a restricted, inaccessible site, the castle was never able to support any kind of township; hence the growth of Llangollen down on the better site beside the River Dee.

Castell Dinas Bran has provided generations of writers with material for extravagant outpourings. H. V. Morton, writing in *In Search of Wales* in 1932, tells the story of Myfanwy Fechan of Dinas Bran, the beautiful but scornful ice maiden who walked abroad 'in scarlet robes with queenly gait, all bowing before her', and of the bard Howell ap Eynion Llygliw, who cried to her in verse:

O bid me sing, as well I may,
Nor scorn my melody in vain,
Or 'neath the walls of Dinas Bran
Behold me perish in my pain.

The fortress of Castell Dinas Bran, located high above modern Llangollen, a poignant expression of the crushed hopes of the Welsh nation in the thirteenth century.

George Borrow, typically, quotes something a good deal more steely from the seventeenth-century bard Roger Cyffyn:

Gone, gone are thy gates, Dinas Bran on the height!
Thy warders are blood-crows and ravens, I trow;
Now no-one will wend from the field of the fight
To the fortress on high, save the raven and crow.

On the very last afternoon of travelling during the writing of this book, a freezing winter's day under threat of snow, I followed in the footsteps of Morton and Borrow up the smooth, slippery slope of the hill to arrive breathless among the ruins. The archway standing on the south side of the hilltop framed a wonderful view down on to Llangollen spread out below, with the Dee winding away beside the slender strip of the canal, the rolling flanks and tops of the Berwyn Hills rising behind. Great peaks and hillsides stretched out towards Snowdonia in the west, snow lying in white patches on their shoulders, topped by grey and yellow snow clouds hurrying out of Wales towards England. On the north-west the Clwydian Hills ran away in their succession of high ridges, while just across the valley rose the slanted bands of alternate orange and grey limestone of Creigiau Eglwyseg. In the east the prospect flattened out, dropping away along the Vale of Llangollen to the vast saucer of the Cheshire plain.

I sat down with my back against the archway and my face towards the Berwyn Hills, thinking back over the long journey – the Wye Valley with its winding cliffs and woods, the long ridges of the remote Black Mountains and the windy spine of Hergest Ridge; the snug black-and-white villages lying low around Ledbury and Leominster, and the cheerful market bustle in beautiful Ludlow; the hard tops of the Clee Hills and the wild moorlands around Kerry; Shrewsbury's tight little island and Newtown filling its valley; the Reverend Donald Carr battling for life in the snowdrifts of the Long Mynd, and George Borrow delighting in his own cleverness at the farmhouse below the Pistyll Rhaeadr waterfall. Gazing out across the hills from Castell Dinas Bran I said goodbye to the Welsh Borders, piece by piece, before picking my way through the first snow flurries back down the hill in gathering darkness to the warmly lit streets of Llangollen.

Looking out from Castell Dinas Bran (OPPOSITE), *the hills and the valleys of the lands along the border between England and Wales stretch away into the far distance.*

Index